C0-AXE-557

THE WAR FILM

A Pyramid Illustrated History of the Movies

by
NORMAN KAGAN

General Editor: **TED SENNETT**

PYRAMID
PUBLICATIONS
NEW YORK

THE WAR FILM
Pyramid Illustrated History of the Movies

First edition published July, 1974

ISBN 0-515-03483-5

Library of Congress Catalog Card Number: 74-1570

Printed in the United States of America

Pyramid Books are published by Pyramid Communications, Inc. Its trademarks, consisting of the word "Pyramid" and the portrayal of a pyramid, are registered in the United States Patent Office.

Pyramid Communications, Inc., 919 Third Avenue, New York, N.Y. 10022

(graphic design by anthony basile)

To my grandfather; Corporal Abraham Negreann,
82nd Division, Company A, 320th Machine Gun Battalion
American Expeditionary Force, 1917-1918

And my grandmother, Minnie Negreann
who knows where the bodies are buried.

ACKNOWLEDGMENTS

I should like to thank the following people for their help and inspiration: Janis Siegel, Steve Lewis, Chris Baffer, Michael Kerbel, Charles Silver, Elizabeth Bodine, Eric Goldman, Earl and Rieselle Schector, Claire Huntington, and my editor, Ted Sennett.

Photographs: Jerry Vermilye, Movie Star News, and The Museum of Modern Art Stills Collection.

CONTENTS

WHAT WE SEE:—A bayonet knife stabs a khaki stomach; a man spurts blood and screams with pain!

—High in the sky, a Zero pilot sniggers: "Okay, you Yankee Doodle Dandy, come up and get us! Where are you gangsters? Come up and get a load of that scrap metal you sold us!"

—A Reb runs into "the red lane of death" to succor a Yank and his foes cheer; a doughboy scampers into No-Man's-Land to help a comrade and is cursed by his sergeant; a G.I. in Korea tries to remove a dead man's dogtags and is blown apart by a hidden grenade; a flier crawls through his plane to help another and watches, helpless and traumatized, while he dies, a victim of "corporate greed" . . .

What do these bright, flashing shadows, to the sounds of tough voices, machines' rumbles, explosions, and dramatic music, have to do with the safe, semi-aware Americans who have watched them in large, darkened halls for over fifty years?

How do all these stylized depictions and calculated stories relate to the rest of the world, and to each other? What do these relationships and patterns tell us?

Today, when the clichés about battle and wartime—as rites of passage, as patriotism, as hidden sadism—seem burned out and exhausted, it is time to consider the

INTRODUCTION: ARE WAR FILMS EVER TRUE?

history of the American war film. The cycles of fifties optimism and alienation, sixties activism and absurdism, and seventies disillusion and disgrace, have purged us and opened new perspectives. (One title I considered was "War Movies: From *The Court-Martial of Billy Mitchell* to *The Court-Martial of Rusty Calley*.")

My approach has been to sort the American fiction films of battle into categories, seeking patterns and meanings, to comment on and question the more popular and critically acclaimed films. But in a sense, all I will be asking and saying is just an expanded reply to the question: Are war films ever true? For we must next ask: true to what?

—*True to war?* What do their depictions of characters and events have to do with the real ones? What is the difference between Sergeant York and *Sergeant York*, and what does it mean? Can we ever film "courage" or "strategy"?

—*True to history?* History is not just the "facts" but principles, explanations, causes and effects. What does *All Quiet On the Western Front* or *The Dirty Dozen* suggest, omit, or falsify about the history of war?

10

—*True to film?* Are there special techniques and conventions for war movies? Are there approaches that lend themselves to such films? What are the tricks, shortcuts and conventions behind the cameras?
—*True to their time?* How do these films reflect the beliefs current when they were made? How do their stories suggest underlying social ideas, motives, and emotions?

—*True to art?* Do the war films' conventions relate to other arts, e.g., the young hero or old warrior types in Renaissance portraiture? In general, how does adaptation reshape a war novel into a war film?

—*True to themselves?* The most treacherous truth of all. Does the war film, by its very subject, straitjacket itself into saying only certain things? What happens when filmmakers set out to "break the rules"?

Of course, bearing all these questions in mind, this study can hardly scratch the surface of this important genre. Yet I believe it does not skip too broadly across it. For now, I am grateful for the chance to plumb the critical depths of a neglected yet fascinating film subject.

D.W. Griffith's *The Birth of a Nation* (1915) and Charlie Chaplin's *Shoulder Arms* (1918) are the *Moby Dick* and the *Huckleberry Finn* of American war films. These two films contain the archetypical themes, plot ideas, story incidents, characters, and cultural assumptions which define the next half century of U.S. combat stories depicted on the screen.

The Birth of a Nation is Griffith's three-hour epic of the Civil War, with the conflicts and tragedies dramatized by showing the changing fortunes of two families: the Camerons of the South and the Stonemans of the North. Like almost all war films, *The Birth of a Nation* professed antiwar sentiments. A title reads: "If in this work we have conveyed to the mind the ravages of war, to the end that war may be held in abhorrence, the effort will not have been in vain." An early scene with the title "Hostilities" shows a scrapping cat and dog, implying that war is a mindless, accidental business men should outgrow. A scene of backlit dead soldiers sprawled on a battlefield is titled: "War's peace."

Yet at the same time, the film shows the preliminaries and garnishments of war as exciting and even inspiring. When the war breaks out, the Southern Cameron boys strut and preen in their new caped uniforms. After the Battle of

TWO CLASSICS: "THE BIRTH OF A NATION" AND "SHOULDER ARMS"

Bull Run, the flag is paraded at a ball while outside the ballroom the crowds celebrate with bonfires.

Aside from its ambivalence about war, *The Birth of a Nation* set the style, the approaches, and the attitudes of many subsequent films on war themes. As the war goes on, the Confederate town of Piedmont becomes shabby, the homes stripped by shortages. When an irregular force of Union guerrillas sweeps in, the animal-like blacks with their scalawag leader assault and bayonet the weak defenders, invading the fine Cameron home, attacking the elderly father with his pitiful flintlock, wrecking and setting the house afire. This image of the swarming of beast-enemies over a fine dwelling containing culture symbols, rightfully defended, shows up in many war films.

The next battle scenes are prefaced: "War claims its bitter, useless sacrifice. True to their promise, the chums meet again." In front of some trees, a young Cameron crouches, runs, is hit and tumbles; a Stoneman races up to bayonet him, hesitates, his rifle raised, his face suddenly split in a grin of recognition—the two boys had met and

THE BIRTH OF A NATION (1915). Sherman's march to the sea

played as teenagers. The same confusion of friends and enemies appears affectingly and perversely in later films.

Following the title: "While women and children weep, a great conquerer marches to the sea," we view a grieving woman and her frightened children beside their burned-out home; then in a distant valley, we see Sherman's troops like ants leaving a swath of bare soil and a flaming cabin. The image appears in countless American war films: the army as a cruel, unstoppable swarm of insects.

After the famous title: "The torch of war against the breast of Atlanta," this concept is embroidered in biblical-like images. Red-tinted, the next shot has two planes of action: in the distance black shadows of buildings against a hellish firestorm, in the foreground people fleeing on foot or in surreys and wagons, lit up by the torches. From a high angle in a harsh dawn, we see a straggling line of refugees strung out across a bleak valley. These compositions have been used again and again over six decades to show desperate and homeless victims of war. We also see how the knowledge of a soldier's death torments his little sister—the first of many children dragged into war movie plots.

The next long sequence begins poetically: "The last great days of the Confederacy. On the battle

THE BIRTH OF A NATION (1915). The "Little Colonel" leads the battle.

THE BIRTH OF A NATION (1915). Captain Stoneman carries the "Little Colonel" to safety.

lines before Petersburg, parched corn their only ration." So when a food convoy is trapped, Lee himself, on a forested promontory like a great stag, orders a breakthrough. As often, the reasons for this movie attack are clear and nonideological.

Griffith begins the combat sequence with a predawn, high-angle view of the devastated battleground, framed by trenches and clumps of trees. An artillery duel is visible in cannon puffs, flashes of discharges, torrents and clouds of glowing smoke. The soldiers fight and flags bob in a thick swarm, half-seen except when flares burst. In this amazing panoramic display of conflict, we see war depicted for the first time as a great spectacle.

The plucky "Little Colonel," Ben Cameron, bright-eyed above his little moustache, wearing long coat, boots, and hat, always swinging his sword, receives his orders in a crowded trench, his men crouching and firing loyally just behind him. Here is the beginning of the American emphasis on the special nature and burden of command rather than the business of killing.

Griffith's skillful exposition continues with a shot of the Union lines, better organized and equipped, the cool, aloof officers standing apart from their men, a little like Nazis—the enemy as cold, regimented, merciless. We see the masked batteries, the artillery complete with horses hitched for a getaway; the mortar pits, all spark-

15

ing our fascination with the "how" of combat.

Now the Little Colonel leads the final, desperate assault against the Union command. Shabby men leap up and run forward; others give covering fire; a few spin to earth at once, in a thrilling cinematic image. The desperate charge plunges forward as the Union soldiers, crouched safely in their trenches, fire ranked rifles systematically.

In closeup, we watch the Little Colonel, eyes mad, mouth screaming, sword swung like a poison wand, short legs pumping, racing forward into the mechanical Union fire, a plucky lone hero leading a few men against the enemy war machine. Along the Union trench, saber, gun, fist, club, and bayonet meet in a dozen hand-to-hand murderous combats. "Two lines of entrenchments taken, but only a remnant of his regiment remains to continue the advance," a title reads. Griffith asks for our sympathy even as his outnumbered little squad of heroes wins, a much-used story device for de-emphasizing national might.

"All hope gone, the Little Colonel pauses before the charge to succor a fallen foe," the next title reads. The Southerner scurries out towards the enemy to bring water to a wounded, gasping Yank. He grins in devil-may-care fashion as the Union men cheer, ducks bug-eyed

at a wild shot, then runs back to his men. This archetypical sequence, the solo rescue of another in no-man's-land, is a standard part of U.S. war movies, its gallantry and optimism declining steadily over the years.

The Little Colonel slaps his hat on, and sword swinging, charges with his surviving men through the high grass—in one moment, one volley, all are hit and fall. He staggers on alone, stars and bars in his arms, rams it in a Union cannon, sprawls before his old friend Captain Stoneman, and is dragged to safety. Griffith's climax is the triple root of almost all war movie highpoints: the gallant but futile last stands, the courageous heroes who finally die to no real purpose, and the irrational, suicidal charges into the face of the enemy.

A title: "In the red lane of death, others take their places, and the battle goes on into the night." Shots of the same battlefield follow, anticipating the conclusion of so many war movies, the mutilated forces moving out to new combat, leaving their dead behind.

Several other sections of *The Birth of a Nation* also seem timeless. The treatment of Piedmont under the scalawags and carpetbaggers has many parallels to American films about occupied countries during World War II. Finally, the Ku Klux Klan activities later and the

THE BIRTH OF A NATION (1915). With Lillian Gish (center)

guerilla raid early on seem to presage many of the ideas in treatments of Vietnam such as *The Green Berets*: the native child instinctively on the right side; the young girl as sexy bait for the depraved enemy leader; the self-righteous "defense" forces.

Like *The Birth of a Nation*, *Shoulder Arms* is a paradigm or model for war films. In the opening sequence, Charlie drills with a squadron in boot camp, only to become entangled by the commands the others follow smartly, and collapses onto a cot. This is the mundane beginning typical of most war films, before they become romantic and/or fantastic.

Title: "Over There". Charlie, loaded down with gear, staggers through the trenches. When a sergeant checks him out, his fingers snap a mousetrap. Corked in the dugout doorway by his equipment, the little fellow is booted through by the sergeant. Meanwhile, in the enemy trenches, a goose-stepping dwarf German officer kicks his men into readiness. The intercutting of brutal foes and nice Yanks was not new, even in 1918, but here is the beginning of the filmic emphasis on command systems, and the tolerance of idiosyncracies (if you can fight!). One can see here the ethnically organized squads and crews to come.

Mail arrives, but Charlie gets none, and refuses bits of his pals' gifts. Instead he tries to read another's letter past his shoulder, revealing his changing emotions in a pathetic display until the man glares and moves away. At last Charlie does get mail—a terrible cheese he must handle wearing a gas mask. At night water fills the dugout, making sleep impossible, so he puffs a floating candle towards the sergeant, giving him a hotfoot. Briefly Chaplin sketches the soldier's frustration, isolation, rebelliousness: the subjects of many future war comedies.

At zero hour, Chaplin heads over the top—only to land in the mud. The next moment he's caught some POWs, including the little officer, whom he spanks. Asked how he did it, he replies: "I surrounded them," laughing at the easy and never explained heroics of war films.

In the next sequence, Charlie manages to obtain a welcome bottle of liquor and a cigarette. He gets the bottle open and his cigarette lit by

SHOULDER ARMS (1918). Charlie has his physical.

SHOULDER ARMS (1918)
Charlie in the army

holding them just above trench level, in the range of enemy sharpshooters. Chaplin chalks up his own bull's-eyes as if he were shooting skeet. When his helmet is shot off, he erases a mark. He volunteers until he's told "you may never return," tries to drop out, is refused and finally goes. This sequence contains the beginnings of the idea of a "private war," an inner-directed soldier hustling by his own rules even in the heat of combat, a great theme of American war movies.

Behind enemy lines, Chaplin is camouflaged as a tree-trunk, the spread of his branches mocking his own shrug. When the Chaplin-tree is menaced by a German looking for firewood with an ax, Charlie kicks the soldier's behind, knocks down two more, and flees. The scene presages the personal style and individuality movie soldiers will bring to battle.

Charlie's sergeant, caught sending back intelligence, is saved by the fleeing tree, which is chased into the woods by a fat German. The two zigzag through, the German bayoneting real trees, Charlie escaping down a sewer that is corked by the fat Kraut. The emphasis here is on American ingenuity, present in nearly every combat film.

Charlie finds the ruin of a house, closing the door although the walls are gone. When a French girl comes to soothe him, he lets her know he's American by shaping an eagle with his fingers, banging his head for "stars," and drawing "stripes." Here is the often-repeated American "respect" for pathetically childlike foreigners, and the instinctive affection of foreign women.

When the Germans arrive, Charlie gives himself up, escaping as the house caves in. On the run, he finds the very command post where the helpless girl is held prisoner, frightens her lascivious warden into a closet, then ducks in himself as the pompous kaiser and strutting crown prince arrive. Seconds later, he comes out in the German's uniform, and takes the girl out, terrified by the sentries' rifles but scratching a match on the kaiser's car. Here is our enemy: a stuffed shirt in public and depraved in private.

The recaptured sergeant shows up, and "German" Charlie roughs him up as he fills him in on events. Moving fast, they slip on German uniforms, Charlie disguising the French girl with a hubcap-grease moustache. Now Charlie chauffeurs the crown prince and kaiser away at full speed—across the Allied lines! Charlie is carried triumphantly on everyone's shoulders—until he wakes up on his cot in boot camp. This sequence, with its notion that the right man at the right time can solve everything, is a dark current running through our war films until the present.

In 1916, films presaging the coming war were melodramatic, sometimes to the point of hysteria, contrasting the worst of war to the best of peace through brutalization of sympathetic, harmless folk. Their content was at best a cry for preparedness, more often a wail of despair building to a scream for vengeance.

Films typifying this attitude included *In the Name of the Prince of Peace* (1916), with a nun denouncing her stormtrooper-invader father, and witnessing his execution at a church altar; *The War Bride's Secret* (1916), with its orgies of German rape and murder, and *On Dangerous Ground* (1917), showing a French girl, humiliated by the kaiser's men, helping a young American escape from occupied France.

Serials, with their ongoing protagonists, tended to accent the positive virtues of preparedness rather than brutalization. *Patria* (1917), financed by William Randolph ("Yellow Peril") Hearst, showed millionairess Irene Castle financing weapons development against Japan and Mexico. *Pearl of the Army* (1916) had Pearl White, the perennial heroine-in-peril, caught up in a duel of wits with Orientals out to blow up our Panama Canal, a tempting target down the years.

As American sympathies for the Allies crested, Cecil B. DeMille

HARBINGERS

turned out two powerful pro-war films. *Joan the Woman* (1916) stylized the saint into a sort of female Spartacus, leading a holy war against her nation's spiritual enemies, implying, as DeMille put it, "an age-old call to a modern crusade." (One later war newsreel was called *Pershing's Crusaders*.) DeMille's *The Little American* (1917) starred Mary Pickford as an American relief worker in neutral Belgium, held as a spy by German troopers depicted as depraved ogres who threatened "America's Sweetheart" with rape and murder. In a bunker at midnight, a Prussian colonel strokes his moustache and intimates, "My men are in need of relaxation." Small wonder the United States declared war on April 17, 1917.

Inevitably, there was a great turning away from the subject of war immediately after the armistice. Yet by the mid-thirties, foreign films were suggesting the conflict to come: *Der Kampf* (*The Struggle*, 1936), made by a Nazi-exiled crew in Russia, showed the Reichstag fire and Dimitroff trial, the terrorizing Brown Shirts, and the concentration camps. *Fight to the Last* (1938),

THE LITTLE AMERICAN (1917). With Mary Pickford (left)

a Chinese film, depicted the Japanese as human fiends, invading the hero's home, shooting his father, ravishing and killing his wife and sister, and bayoneting his son.

Perhaps the first American film on the subject was *Hitler's Reign of Terror* (1934), which encountered almost as many censorship problems in the U.S. as in the Reich.

Independently produced, *I Was a Captive of Nazi Germany* (1936), enacted by the captive herself and "an anonymous cast," included race persecution, book burnings, and concentration camp torture, but was laughed off by a *New York Times* reviewer as: "less an exposé of Nazi persecution than a mirror for . . . rather amazing unsophisti-

cation."* In fact as late as May 1941, Germany's *Sieg in Westen* (*Victory in the West*, 1941), played in York-ville and indeed: "the applause in the theatre is amazing. Hitler naturally draws the most applause, but there is plenty for parachutists, dive-bomber pilots, and advance guards."**

Hollywood's fiction films anticipating the Second World War were more intelligent and controlled, as well as far better made, than the forerunners of the First. These films tended to follow public opinion rather than lead it, using the

The New York Times, August 3, 1936.
**R.R. Lingeman, *Don't You Know There's a War On?*, New York, G.P. Putnam's Sons, 1970, p. 172.

THE LAST TRAIN FROM MADRID (1937). With Anthony Quinn and Dorothy Lamour

topicality of the expanding war without taking a strong stand. *The Last Train From Madrid* (1938), concerning refugees caught up in the fury of the Spanish Civil War, used a political escapee's plight and flight to generate suspense and romantic heat without saying much about what the factions actually stood for. *Blockade* (1938), had Henry Fonda as a Spanish farmer who joins his nation's struggle against enemies who bombed civilians and villages. The tone of the film is very uneven, switching from a spy story involving Madeleine Carroll to musical interludes in Spanish cabarets to scenes of destruction as modern weapons smash towns and lives. A strong conclusion has the enemy forces temporarily stymied, and Fonda making a plea to the "conscience of the world" for help. Still, *Blockade* condemned the Fascists by implication and was banned in Nazi countries and picketed here.

Confessions of a Nazi Spy (1939) was the first real anti-Nazi film from an American studio. Based on the 1938 spy trials, the film's quasi-documentary format stated that German embassies and consulates were the command posts of a

BLOCKADE (1938). With Madeleine Carroll and Henry Fonda

CONFESSIONS OF A NAZI SPY (1939). With Paul Lukas and Edward G. Robinson

THE MORTAL STORM (1940). With Maria Ouspenskaya, Bonita Granville, and Margaret Sullavan

hidden war already being waged, and utilized newsreel footage of Hitler and his Brown Shirts. Edward G. Robinson was highly effective as the G-man, filmed against an American flag, or in actual defense-plant locations. Though the film had ferocious energy, the *New York Times* critic complained that he doubted that "Nazi propaganda ministers let their mouths twitch evilly whenever they mention our Constitution or Bill of Rights." Follow-ups using this pseudo-documentary approach included *Beast of Berlin* (1939) and *Underground* (1941), showing an anti-Reich underground complete with cellar printing presses, leaflets, midnight searches, and double agents.

A third sort of early dramatization of Nazi villainy was the high-level melodrama in which the characters had more depth: *Four Sons, The Mortal Storm,* and *Escape.* In *Four Sons* (1940), we see the mutilation of a Czech family by National Socialism: brothers Alan Curtis and Don Ameche are killed on opposite sides when the Reich invades, young George Ernest dies fighting in Poland, and mother Eugenie Leontovich flees to America to join her surviving son, Robert Lowery. *The Mortal Storm* (1940) showed the impact of the war on a German family in 1933, when the Nazi takeover turns their quiet university town into a nightmare of deception and brutality. Father-professor

FOREIGN CORRESPONDENT (1940). The plane crash at sea, with (left to right) Joel McCrea, Gertrude Hoffman, George Sanders, Laraine Day, and Herbert Marshall

I WANTED WINGS (1941). With Ray Milland, Wayne Morris, and William Holden

Frank Morgan ends up in a concentration camp for insisting "race blood types" are nonsense; his two stepsons Robert Stack and William Orr are transformed into stormtroopers, and defiant daughter Margaret Sullavan resists the Nazis and is then shot down at the border with fiancé James Stewart. *Escape* (1940) has young American Robert Taylor return to Germany to smuggle his mother (Alla Nazimova) out of a concentration camp.

After 1940, films anticipating the war often put their protagonists into at least semimilitary roles on the Allied side. Alfred Hitchcock's *Foreign Correspondent* (1940), tipped newshawk Joel McCrea into fifth column intrigue, the rescue of a Dutch patriot, and a struggle with Nazi agents. This film turned a private citizen into what amounted to an OSS operative, who, aware of the facts, pleaded for American preparedness from a blitzkrieged London: "before the lights go out." Fritz Lang's *Man Hunt* (1941), takes this particular approach to its limit with British game-hunter Walter Pidgeon who, "purely for sport," goes to Germany before the war to see if he can bag the Fuehrer. With Adolf in his sights, debating whether or not to fire, he is grabbed by the Gestapo, and the rest of the film is a critique of Nazism until Pigeon joins the army to fight the enemy in a more conventional way. *A Yank in the RAF* (1941), made with British help, is a film about clean-cut young Tyrone Power who ferries a bomber to England strictly for the money, meets old-flame dancer Betty Grable, joins the RAF merely to stay around, and then is converted to the Allied cause by participating in bomber raids and the retreat from Dunkirk, the sky full of huge dark bombers and shark-bellied Spitfires. For obvious reasons, the British changed the ending from death in the blitz to a happy fadeout of Power with Grable.

A flock of early forties service melodramas were notable for the way they minimized the hazards and glorified the camaraderie of military life, as well as being promotions for new multimillion-dollar lethal hardware: *Parachute Battalion* (1940) of aerial troop deployment, *I Wanted Wings* (1941) of the new B-17s, *Flight Command* (1941) of carrier planes, *Navy Blues* (1941) of gunnery, and *Dive Bomber* (1941) of flight safety systems.

This sequence of melodramas, pseudo- and semi-documentaries,

MAN HUNT (1941). With Joan Bennett and Walter Pidgeon

atrocity stories, and showcases for weaponry appeared for a third time, following the declaration of the Cold War in the Truman Doctrine of 1947. *The Iron Curtain* (1948) used the time-tested form of the spy pseudo-documentary to portray the Communists as supergangsters with a mad lust to destroy us. *Whip Hand* (1951) had a Soviet-run U.S. prison camp where biological warfare weapons were field-tested on Mr. and Mrs. John Q. Public, *I Was a Communist for the FBI* (1951) detailed methods of Soviet subversion. *Big Jim McLain* (1952) showed the same John Wayne who had fought in World War II films hunting Commies in Hawaii. Finally, films like *Bombers B-52* (1957) and *Strategic Air Command* (1955) were modeled on the service dramas of 1941, with their cheerful fliers and spectacular weaponry courtesy of Uncle Sam. In *Strategic Air Command*, James Stewart is a big-league ballplayer called back to the H-bomb patrol that guards America, with June Allyson as his perfect wife. But *The New York Times* review showed how little things had changed from 1917: "Above all, there are those airplanes, the roaring engines, the cluttered cockpits, the clouds and sky. These are the things that make your eyes bug and your heart leap with wonder and pride."

Fortunately, this third sequence of harbingers was not a self-fulfilling prophecy . . .

When the United States entered World War I, peace films were forbidden by government order. (The producer of *The Spirit of '76* [1918], which allegedly gave aid and comfort to the enemy, was sentenced to ten years in prison under the Espionage Act.) Instead Congress established a Committee of Public Information to "sell the war" to the public. At first limited to straight propaganda documentaries like *Pershing's Crusaders*, *America's Answer,* and *Under Two Flags* (all 1918), by the close of the war the Committee was handing the studios ideas, scripts, troops for extras, bases and other facilities for locations, free promotion, and sometimes even production money.

Almost as soon as Wilson made his declaration, wartime features flooded into the theaters. A great many were aimed at shifting public opinion: *Shame* (1917) and *The Slacker* (1917) preached against draft dodging; *Too Fat to Fight* (1917) and *Eighteen to Forty-Five* (1917) boosted enlisting; *The Hun Within* (1918) and *War and the Woman* (1918) justified informing; others exhorted people to work harder, conserve food, and accept the loss of loved ones. Though, except for Griffith, no working filmmaker ever got to the front, they persisted in hammering across their point with spectacular battle climaxes, from which (because he

FILMS OF WORLD WAR I

volunteered, or his family skipped lunches), the hero emerged unscathed and returned to his loved ones.

There were few serious story films about combat made during the war, and for a number of years afterwards. The reasons probably included revulsion with the subject and the wish to enjoy the post-war boom without guilt or remorse. (A similar but shorter timelag occurred after World War II.) There were exceptions: *Behind the Door* (1919) accurately depicted submarine warfare, with a Navy skipper revenging himself on a U-boat captain who killed his wife by skinning him alive!; *The Four Horsemen of the Apocalypse* (1921) starred Valentino as a Franco-Brazilian aroused by love and compassion to join the French forces and fight to the death in spectacular, well-staged battle scenes.

The first important film about the Great War was King Vidor's *The Big Parade* (1925). Its hero, James Apperson (John Gilbert), something of a playboy, volunteers on impulse but fits right in, brawling cheerfully and chewing gum, making friends with an ex-riveter.

THE BIG PARADE (1925). With Renee Adoree and John Gilbert

THE BIG PARADE (1925). With Tom O'Brien, John Gilbert, and Karl Dane

And he dallies with an independent French peasant girl (Renée Adorée), who rushes frantically after his departing truck, clinging to him until the last moment in a well-remembered scene. The regiments, caissons, and trucks depart at a brisk pace, but a foreboding slowness ensues before a strafing attack. Similarly, at Belleau Woods, as a machine gun thins the ranks, each part of the advance is filmed at a different cadence, declining into the ultimate loneliness of combat. Later scenes in the trenches show the riveter as a sharpshooter who collects tin hats in place of scalps or skins, pioneer-style. But when Apperson tries to rescue his friend from No-Man's Land, he ends up helping a wounded enemy instead. Losing a leg in the war, Apperson, encouraged by his mother, hobbles back to France to marry the willful but loving peasant girl.

Director King Vidor described his goal this way: "A man walks through the war and looks at it, neither a pacifist nor a soldier, he simply goes through, and has a look, and is pulled into these experiences." The film's craftsmanship, strong action sequences, sentimental optimism and perhaps lack of moralizing made it a tremendous success. Raymond Durgnat has suggested that the real core of its power is a sort of "vitalism" of the characters, responding to and affirming each other. He also supposes why the No-Man's-Land rescue has become a Hollywood cliché: "a guarantee that the hero's acceptance of authority has not crushed his independent individualism."* I would add that this is also about the only solo romantic self-assertive act possible in combat; (and so important that the anti-war *All Quiet On the Western Front* [1930] battle sequences

*Raymond Durgnat, "King Vidor," in *Film Comment*, July 1973, p. 11

start out by bitterly debunking it). Critically attacked for its sentimentality, *The Big Parade's* success showed there are many ways of looking at war, and indicated how the romantic view of war may predominate several years after the smoke has cleared.

The Big Parade was made partly to "scoop" Raoul Walsh's *What Price Glory* (1926), an adaptation of the Maxwell Anderson play showing war as the boisterous competition of comrades-at-arms Victor McLaglen and Edmund Lowe. Belleau Woods and other engagements were masterfully staged, with scenes of night combat made more powerful by being only half-visible in the blaze from flares

WHAT PRICE GLORY? (1926). With Dolores Del Rio and Victor McLaglen

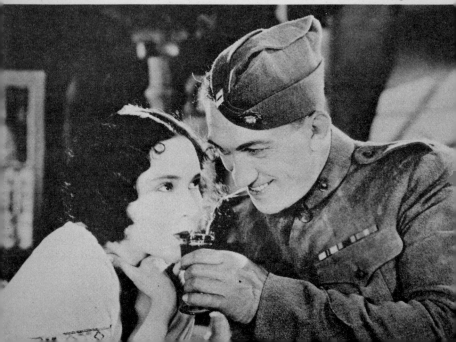

WINGS (1927). With Richard Arlen (center)

as the troops stumble forward or fall. One great effect is the "Trench of Death"—a bomb explosion that destroys scores of soldiers huddling for protection. Eileen Bowser has noted that the film reflected increasing honesty in films. "Heroes actually swore, . . . got drunk, whored, fought among themselves . . . the heroine is clearly shown to be a camp follower . . . bawdiness is emphasized by close shots of buttocks, legs, and half-bared shoulders."**

**Eileen Bowser, *Film Notes*, Museum of Modern Art, New York, 1969

After *Behind the Door* (1919), there were virtually no films on Navy combat until *Convoy* turned up in 1925 with the destroyer vs. U-boat plot that became standard for many of these films. All the trappings were there, already full-grown: the lifting and dropping periscope, torpedo wakes, destroyers plunging along dropping depth charges, and submarine wolfpacks attacking a helpless passenger liner. Period reviewers singled out for praise the sequence of a destroyer being hit, going over on its side, turning turtle, and going under.

HELL'S ANGELS (1930). With Douglas Gilmore and Jean Harlow

The romance, gallantry, and visual excitement of sky warfare produced a steady stream of aerial combat films through the late twenties and thirties, inspired by William Wellman's *Wings* (1927), one of the best air-war movies ever made. Buddy Rogers and Richard Arlen are aviators who love the same nurse (Clara Bow). Arlen crashes behind enemy lines, steals a Fokker, tries to fly home, but is shot down by his pal. Perhaps the best sequence is Rogers' half-crazed treetop-strafing run over the enemy trenches during a big push, the bullets making ranked troops leap off the road,

sending a staff car into a ditch, setting a barrage balloon afire. For the silent version of this film, theaters had whirring motors roar behind the screen for the takeoffs, and a doleful, falling siren whine for the crashes.

It was the thrills and terror of the dogfights, the bombings, the recons, and spectacular crashes that made *Wings* a rousing action adventure, as well as the men's personal and professional gallantry and mutual affection. In addition to the battle excitement, one feels the crazy wonder of open-cockpit flight itself, probably the closest experience to the dream of flight, of being a true "bird man"—a bright-colored, powerful, sky-animal, driven by tireless muscle-motors, romping and racing and fighting high in space, while soldiers grub around in the mud below. So if the planes strafe or bomb, it's not really morality, but evolution, and a crash is terrible, like an angel's death.

Hell's Angels (1930) was a second great air-war film, particularly praised for its Zeppelin and bombing episodes. We first see the Zeppelin prowling the night clouds, its great interiors and motors, the spectacular but futile bombing (the English-born bombardier misdirects them), the desperate defense in which equipment is jetisoned, then officers leap stiffly to doom "For Kaiser and Fatherland!" Finally, a British plane dives into the great warship, causing it to fall in a colossal pyre, metal ribs melting. Another sequence, with Ben Lyon and James Hall as brothers flying an enemy plane to wipe out a munitions dump, then fighting off von Richthofen's air circus as they run for their own lines, is also thrilling.

Howard Hawks' highly re-

THE DAWN PATROL (1930). With Douglas Fairbanks, Jr. and Richard Barthelmess

garded *The Dawn Patrol* (1930, remade in 1938 under Edmund Goulding's direction), is the last of the famous air-war films, again honored for its spectacular dog fights, cruising air fleets, and munitions dump knockout. The story has fliers Courtney (Richard Barthelmess) and Scott (Douglas Fairbanks, Jr.) at odds with boss Major Brand (Neil Hamilton). When they wipe out an enemy air fleet on the ground, Courtney gets Brand's soul-rotting job of ordering men to death and is soon forced to send Scott's brother on a one-way mission. Their friendship broken, Scott volunteers to hit a munitions dump, a suicidal assignment. Courtney drinks him under the table, then goes himself; Scott becomes the new officer-in-charge.

Though it was called an antiwar film, it is hardly that because the characters suffer in a social vacuum, almost masochistically. Like the frustrated cop in *Dirty Harry* or the obsessed rangehand in *The Searchers*, their anguish has a glamorous, aristocratic, nearly perverted side—*this* is the way to go! Besides, they're so happy in the sky! This becomes clear in the 1938 version, with the same spectacles (sometimes the same footage) and the same story—but with a healthier, jauntier Courtney (Errol Flynn) and an irrepressible Scott (David Niven) making *The Dawn Patrol* (1938), in a phrase of the day, "an advert for the preparedness boys."

It was the aristocratic complexities and adolescent tensions of the air war, a vestigial gallantry hanging on in an age of mass slaughter, that kept films on the subject interesting, as the writers and directors explored new meanings in its dependably thrilling iconography. *The Last Flight* (1932) was a sort of *Tender is the Night* of the birdmen, with four sensitive postwar pilots drifting around Europe, three into self-destruction, one "saved" by a perceptive, quirky flapper. *Sky Devils* (1932) seems to have been a World War I *Catch-22:* war as a crazy picnic, the half-mad flyers bombing Germans and Allies alike, one admitting he'd shot down so many of his own planes that he was practically an enemy ace, others flying away to land in what they think is neutral Switzerland, triumphant at the sound of yodeling, then finding it's coming from a German pilot's phonograph! *The Eagle and the Hawk* (1932) was a sincere anti-war study, with Fredric March as a pilot tortured by the loss of his men, going on leave, forced to listen to endless, ignorant prattle about the glamour of war (except from an understanding Carole Lombard), returning to see more deaths, and finally destroying himself. *Lucky Devils* (1932) and

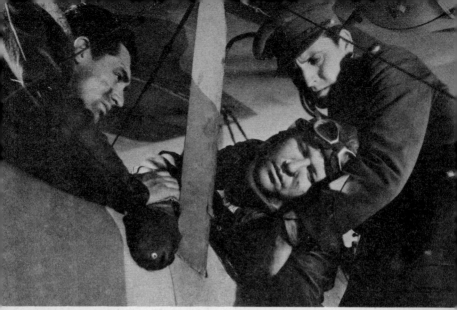

THE EAGLE AND THE HAWK (1933). With Cary Grant, Jack Oakie, and Fredric March

THE FIGHTING 69th (1939). With Pat O'Brien and James Cagney

The Lost Squadron (1933) blurred fact and fiction, showing the unwanted, frustrated aces working in Hollywood, where the actual wartime trappings are duplicated, even the blackboard with the erased names of fallen buddies. (Commandant Erich von Stroheim in *Crimson Romance* [1934] calls this "flying as a problem in simple subtraction.") In *The Devil's Squadron* (1936), the same bitter birdmen, like ex-athletes hooked on a murderous sport, work as test pilots risking the "9-G Dive" required for government certification of new aircraft.

As new war clouds gathered, *La Grande Illusion (Grand Illusion)*, (1937) used a World War I story as a plea for peace, but two other important films used the same background to stress preparedness: *The Fighting 69th* (1940) and *Sergeant York* (1941). *The Fighting 69th* had Cagney's frisky, tough Brooklyn Private Plunkett joining Manhattan's famous "Fighting Irish" regiment, even as he jeers at its traditions, chaplain, and colonel. He feuds with everyone during training but at the front, real corpses, No Man's Land, and an enemy "he can't get his hands on" scare Plunkett into hysteria so that he lets the enemy know their position, causing great losses. Finally bolstered by Chaplain Duffy (Pat O'Brien), he redeems himself with bravery that costs him his life. Critics agreed it was hard to take this film seriously, but complimented Cagney and O'Brien on their vigorous performances.

Howard Hawks' film, *Sergeant York* (1941), appearing when war looked even more of a certainty, was an attempt to show the motivations and character of the greatest hero of the Great War, a pacifist whose real hope was to have the guns stop. York (Gary Cooper) is a poor Tennessee farmer who yearns for a fertile "piece of bottom," gets religion but after a spiritual ordeal ("War's ag'in the Book"), joins up when an officer convinces him there are times when a man has no choices but to fight for his country. Seeing the carnage in the American trenches, York uses his mountain tricks like a "turkey gobble" to lure the Germans to show their heads. In the Battle of the Argonne, he single-handedly captures 132 enemy soldiers, is decorated by the president, and returns to his girl and humble farm.

Reviewers praised the film for being both serious and timely, perhaps helping Americans decide where their own duty lay. Though it seems slick today, the first half was noted for its great power, and for images like "primitivist" American paintings.

The wartime musical *Yankee Doodle Dandy* (1942) had Cagney as

SERGEANT YORK (1941). With George Tobias, Gary Cooper, and Joe Sawyer

George M. Cohan, celebrating the earlier conflict and building American morale worldwide. From then on World War II monopolized the box office until *Paths of Glory* (1957), *King and Country* (1968), and *Oh! What a Lovely War* (1969), all well-made, stylized anti-war films set in World War I. Wellman's *Lafayette Escadrille* (1958) was an unsuccessful attempt to continue the birdman epics of the twenties and thirties.

A more successful film was *The Blue Max* (1966), directed by John Guillermin. *The Blue Max* was Germany's highest flying medal, given for twenty kills. A young fighter pilot named Bruno Stachel (George Peppard) will do anything to get it. He even maneuvers a fellow pilot's plane into crashing, to grab two of his kills. He also takes the dead pilot's mistress Kaeti (Ursula Andress), wife of a count (James Mason), who wants his pilots to win at any cost. With German defeat certain, his kills being investigated, but the Blue Max in sight, Bruno refuses Kaeti's plea to flee, so she tells all. But the count won't have his "people's hero" disgraced, and has him test-fly a faulty plane, performing fantastic maneuvers and then crashing, to die a martyr.

Most critics praised the film, though as usual in the genre, they found the earthbound sequences tedious (i.e., the planes stole the

41

THE BLUE MAX (1966). With Ursula Andress and James Mason

show). The slow exposure of Stachel's rottenness was disapproved, like a bad joke on the traditional sensitive ace who is slowly going crazy; moreover his "brave death," involving hypocrisy by all concerned, hardly works as redemption, but further kills viewer sympathy. Perhaps it would have been best if Stachel stayed the hateful, murderous, alcoholic, blackmailing, class-climbing bad-hat of the novel, instead of having the adapters follow the Hollywood rule that a hero-heel must be boyish, winning, and a terror abed.

Roger Corman's *Von Richthofen and Brown* (1971) is the most recent attempt to portray the sky knights, paralleling the careers of von Richthofen (John Philip Law), the Prussian aristocrat, and Roy Brown (Don Stroud), a Canadian farmer-pilot who downs him. Despite its aerial battles, *Von Richthofen and Brown* is, in many ways a sort of philosophical reflection on the passing of an era. All aspects of von Richthofen's noble background are emphasized: his wealthy landholding family, his proud father who believes things will soon return to the nine-

VON RICHTHOFEN AND BROWN (1971). With Hurd Hatfield and John Philip Law

teenth century, his ceremonial removing of the insignia from his kills, his poetic viewpoint: "Every moment I'm in the air with those Spandaus, in my hands—that's forever." Farmer Brown is a lower-class type who just hates the war and wants it over, thinking of himself as a technician: "I change things. Put a man and a plane in front of me, and I change them into a wreck and a corpse." Yet even he begins to see that this war is very special. He realizes "we have to pretend to go mad (to keep from really going mad)." And when the dead Baron's red Fokker comes in to make an almost perfect landing in a green field, the irrevocable social and spiritual transformations of this war seem not so much stressed, as sealed.

With America's entry into the Great War, films about our allies and enemies increased dramatically. Several films featured American citizens in the battle zone. In *A Soul in Pawn* (1917), beautiful Gail King becomes a spy to repay the Germans who murdered her husband. In *The Greatest Power* (1917), Ethel Barrymore turns against her lover when it is revealed he is a Prussian agent.

Atrocity films multiplied quickly, with increasing emphasis on brutality. In *Bitter Sweet* (1917), fourteen-year-old Ella Hall escapes to the United States after enduring the unspeakable. *The Belgian* (1917) showed the country's underground's defiance coming to naught. *Till I Come Back to You* (1918) depicted Belgian children shipped to Germany to work in munitions factories where they are whipped, starved, and brainwashed. A more modulated work which dwelt on the hardships of civilians was Griffith's *Hearts of the World* (1919), the love story of French girl Lillian Gish whose village is overrun by German troops; it featured a last-minute rescue by her soldier-fiancé. Outstanding were the backgrounds of actual destroyed French towns and villages where Griffith shot much of the film (with Allied cooperation). One haunting moment showed a stunned Gish wandering through the ruins carrying her wedding dress in her arms.

FRIENDS AND ENEMIES

A third type of war drama lampooned the Kaiser, exploiting the grotesque visual humor of his pointy mustache, goggle-eyed leer, pudgy build, elaborate uniforms, and spear-topped helmet, while characterizing him as lustful, crude, conceited, and half-insane. *The Kaiser, Beast of Berlin* (1918) turned the leader of a great nation into a syphilitic and monstrous cartoon, while *To Hell with the Kaiser* (1918) showed the devil as a sort of Kaiser's Kissinger, advising the torpedoing of civilian ships, poison gas attacks, and the bombing of hospitals. *The Kaiser's Finish* (1918) advocated publicly hanging him in Times Square, while *America Must Conquer* (1918) said that any German leaders not shot should be sterilized. *Daughter of Destiny* (1918) and *After the War* (1918) showed the extermination of the imperial family and the execution of the entire German general staff as desirable.

After the Japanese attack in December 1941, the first films showed the confusion, anger, patriotic stirrings and other gut feelings of the ordinary citizen. In spy and sabo-

SABOTEUR (1942). With Robert Cummings and Priscilla Lane

tage thrillers, American civilians were pressured and tortured (*Joe Smith, American.* 1942) terrorized and pursued (*Saboteur,* 1942), and even blackmailed by evil twin brothers (*Nazi Agent,* 1942), before they totalled platoons of well-trained enemy agents. Films like *All Through the Night* (1941) and *Lucky Jordan* (1943) showed even shady citizens like gangster Humphrey Bogart and racketeer Alan Ladd as potential patriots who would know what to do when they had a Nazi in their sights.

A second sort of film gave approving portraits of our allies. *Spitfire* (1943) told the story of the plane's designer, spurred on by Nazi boasts, sacrificing health and life to

MRS. MINIVER (1942). With Greer Garson and Walter Pidgeon

build a better pursuit ship. *Journey for Margaret* (1942) was about two of Britain's homeless shell-shocked children, adopted and brought to the United States by an American journalist. It presented many scenes of blitzed and defiant England.

Mrs. Miniver (1942), directed by William Wyler, was perhaps the most important film about our allies. We see the attractive upper-class British Miniver family (Walter Pidgeon, Greer Garson, and children), in an idyllic countryside England, the war approaching in hints. During the course of the film, their home is smashed, Walter Pidgeon and his motor launch help the Dunkirk evacuation, Greer Garson cap-

MISSION TO MOSCOW (1943). With Walter Huston and Ann Harding

tures a downed German pilot, their town is blitzed, and their upper-class daughter-in-law (Teresa Wright) is killed in a bombing raid. The film ends on an upbeat note in a church service—viewed through a hole in the chapel roof. Spitfires, one piloted by Miniver Junior, are headed into combat.

Recent critics have called *Mrs. Miniver* beautifully crafted propaganda, with its careful muting of national flaws and its calculatedly attractive but slightly smug characters who encourage our resentment and envy, which their war experiences transform to real affection and admiration for their courage, Hemingway's "grace under pressure." Yet even today, only the forewarned or sophisticated can resist *Mrs. Miniver*. Perhaps its attraction now is the way it shows a war fought with a clear conscience, an "honest" war, probably the last we shall ever know.

Michael Curtiz's *Mission to Moscow* (1943) is an interesting parallel, painting approving portraits of our new Communist ally from Ivan to

Stalin. The Moscow trials of the 1930s are excused as a purge of Trotskyite traitors working with Berlin and Tokyo to weaken Mother Russia, the seizing of half of Finland as taking a few defense outposts, and British and French envoys are shown as ineffectual and defeatist. *Song of Russia* (1944) and *Days of Glory* (1944) were similar products of the "Soviet honeymoon."

At the height of the war, depictions of the enemy rose to lunatic levels. *Hitler's Children* (1943) was boy-meets-girl Nazi-style, with a German-American youth (Tim Holt) headed for the General Staff and an American-German girl (Bonita Granville) bound for sterilization because of her non-Aryan chromosomes. The film's sets included an indoctrination camp and sterilizing room, populated by *Hitler jugend* whose fanaticism eerily resembles the faith of Hare Krishna and Maharaji Ji followers. *The Hitler Gang* (1944) was a quasi-documentary of the rise of the Nazi movement, beginning with a paranoid Corporal Hitler convalescing in 1918, who more or less remains a maniac, teamed with a fawning Goebbels, a swishy Roehm, a drug-ridden Goering, through the 1934 Brown Shirt purge. Despite the meticulously accurate Hollywood sets, the film seemed to be a comic-book guide to current events, showing history shaped by troubled minds. By exclusion and emphasis, it denied the

HITLER'S CHILDREN (1943). With Tim Holt (left) and Bonita Granville

THE SEVENTH CROSS (1944). With Spencer Tracy and Signe Hasso

monstrous deeds and power of these men, making them seem more the four evil stooges rather than a major threat to world sanity and survival.

Perhaps the most moving and effective film about the enemy was *The Seventh Cross* (1944), directed by Fred Zinnemann. Spencer Tracy, fleeing from a concentration camp, sees his six companions hunted down and sacrificed by Hitler's followers—hung on six trees stripped of their bark while a seventh waits empty. Loved ones betray him, but a few tough people have not surrendered to the black regime, and their decency stands for a human spirit which will not be defeated. *Behind the Rising Sun* (1943) showed the other side of the coin, with a young Japanese who had studied in America being slowly transformed into a fanatic Tojoist.

The German occupation of Europe attracted filmmakers as a ready source of color, conflict, and confrontation. *The Moon is Down* (1943) showed the garrisoning of a Norwegian village, with John Steinbeck's free and noble people refusing to be suppressed even by Nazi commandant Sir Cedric Hardwicke. Yet the *too* philosophical Norwegians' resistance was not dramatically convincing. *Edge of Darkness* (1943) had Errol Flynn, Ann Sheridan and a reluctant but finally aggressive Walter Hus-

ton leading another Norwegian resistance, but its action-film approach worked. Beginning with a German patrol finding the demolished village which still defiantly flies a Norwegian flag, it proceeded through flashbacks to a climactic, spectacular Norse vs. Nazis battle. *Hangmen Also Die* (1943) had the Czech underground assassinate their Reich Protector, then handing over a "Quisling" from their own ranks to the Gestapo, with faked evidence to show he's the killer. Fast pacing and an authentic-looking milieu helped to gloss over one's doubt that the SS would fall for this stunt. Jean Renoir's *This Land is Mine* (1943) had timid schoolmaster Charles Laughton make a defiant speech to his Nazi conquerors, while *North Star* (1943), written by playwright Lillian Hellman, showed Russian peasants Farley Granger, Anne Baxter, Walter Brennan, and Walter Huston resisting the German heel, including SS Doctor Erich von Stroheim who uses Soviet children as a sort of blood bank. *Dragon Seed* (1944) depicted a not-very-convincingly Oriental Katharine Hepburn leading the peace-loving Chinese fight against the Japanese invaders. Her efforts include having the farmers set their crops afire rather than letting them be confiscated. In a spectacular finale, a Japanese victory banquet becomes the scene of a mass execution, with hundreds of poisoned Rising Sun officers writhing in agony.

Alfred Hitchcock's *Lifeboat* (1944) was a carefully worked out variation on the occupation theme. It depicted a freighter's assorted Allied nationals—haughty Tallulah Bankhead, tough John Hodiak, wealthy Henry Hull, wounded William Bendix, and others—drifting in the rescue craft with a U-boat captain (suave Walter Skezak) after both ships have destroyed each other. The *unterboaten-kommandant* is charming, competent, resourceful, but treacherous and inhuman. Yet the Nazi winds up taking command as the others give in, and only their horror when he dumps Bendix overboard saves them from a concentration camp as they instinctively bludgeon Slezak to death. In the end, they seem to find a new "motor" among themselves. Hitchcock said he had scenarist Jo Swerling, drawing on a John Steinbeck story, make his Nazi a strong character to show the Nazis should not be underestimated.

THE NORTH STAR (1943). With (left to right) Dana Andrews, Jane Withers, Eric Roberts, Anne Baxter, and Farley Granger

LIFEBOAT (1944). With (left to right) Henry Hull, John Hodiak, Hume Cronyn, Tallulah Bankhead, and Mary Anderson

Post-1945 films about our World War II friends and enemies have mostly continued the themes and viewpoints expressed in the early forties. In recent years there have been many about Nazi society, perhaps inspired by our own feelings of decadence and decay. Visconti's *The Damned* (1971), the most voluptuously spectacular, shows the Third Reich founded on transvestism, criminal opportunism, child-molesting, matricidal rape, incest, and drug addiction among Germany's foremost families. *The Conformist* (1972) suggests Fascism is repressed homosexuality; *Cabaret* (1972) says it feeds on a frantic hedonism. Only *England Made Me* (1973) suggests economic as well as cultural factors for the drift downward, with its depiction of amoral big business trying to ride the Nazi tiger.

Films about the Occupation also continue. *The Train* (1965) concerns French underground fighter Burt Lancaster saving a trainload of art

53

treasures from the Reich, and *The Heroes of Telemark* (1968) depicts Norwegian resistance fighters wiping out a Nazi heavy-water plant; both films were action-adventures. But others like *The Diary of Anne Frank* (1959) and *The Shop on Main Street* (1966) were devastating pictures of the consequences of war on people, the last showing a Slovak misfit, the "Aryan companion" of an ancient Jewess of whom he becomes fond, trying vainly to save her from the death camps.

There have been relatively few films about our new friends and enemies in the Cold War. The comforting *The Desert Fox* (1951), *The Sea Chase* (1955), and *The Enemy Below* (1957) show the German military as brave and anti-Hitler. The early television drama about the Soviet leaders, Playhouse 90's "The Plot to Kill Stalin" (1954), was eerily similar to *The Hitler Gang* with its megalomaniac commissars including triggerman Khrushchev like a dwarfted, hateful, squinting "Mr. Clean", his mole the size of a silver dollar. Kubrick's *Dr. Strangelove* (1964) suggested the Russian premier was a drunken, lecherous child, while leaving him discreetly off-screen. *Che!* (1969) implied that Jack Palance's Castro was canny enough not to provoke Uncle Sam, and only Omar Sharif's revolution-exporting Che was dangerously unbalanced.

There have been almost no films about the Communist-occupied nations, especially those nonwhites living under the Red flag. There are many reasons for this: lack of U.S. interest in, and audience identification with, Asiatic peoples; no resistance movements to dramatize; the difficulty of illustrating civics-book differences between Soviet control, native mores, and the American presence. The few films on this subject, *The Quiet American* (1958) and *The Ugly American* (1963), have at least suggested our weaknesses abroad.

THE DAMNED (1970). With Dirk Bogarde and Ingrid Thulin

CHE! (1969), In foreground: Linda Marsh, Omar Sharif and Woody Strode

In Hollywood the response to Pearl Harbor was swift and sure. Almost at once such titles as *Yellow Peril*, *The Stolen Bombsight*, *Wings Over the Pacific*, *Sunday in Hawaii*, and *V for Victory* were copyrighted. Because sound stages looked like airplane factories, Jack Warner had a twenty-foot east-pointing arrow painted atop his studio with the inscription:

LOCKHEED—THATAWAY→

Again, the United States appointed a Coordinator of Motion Pictures, the industry itself eager for coordination rather than a low-priority "non-essential" slow death. By August 1942, a *Government Information Manual for the Motion Pictures* was making the rounds.

Strictly speaking, the first true war story was *A Yank On the Burma Road* (1942), rushed through to completion only seven weeks after the bombing. It starred Barry Nelson as a tough New York hackie who trades his taxicab job for pushing a supply truck in the Far East "strictly for the money," then finds himself cursing the Japanese treachery as he speeds and bulls a Chinese convoy of supplies through to rescue an embattled outpost. Thought frivolous by some, it did show a positive "can-do" American response to the Pacific holocaust.

Most other early releases dealing

FILMS OF WORLD WAR II

with war were "preparedness operas," a few hastily updated. *The Bugle Sounds* (1942) showed old cavalry sergeant Wallace Beery swapping his charger for an armored vehicle, and capturing a band of saboteurs in the bargain. *Eagle Squadron* (1942) made Robert Stack a U.S. pilot in the RAF who hijacks an experimental Nazi plane in a commando raid; in *Captains of the Clouds* (1942), James Cagney joins the Royal Canadian Air Force, winning his wings and finally ferrying a bomber to England, where, gunless, he whips a Nazi raider off the English coast. *Flying Tigers* (1942) brought John Wayne to Chenault's early-on war in Manchuria, with "Duke" shooting down Zeros and bombing Jap bridges by dropping nitro at zero altitude.

Hollywood's approach to our war effort was confirmed in the first important action-combat film, *Wake Island* (1942). This movie, the first of the "last stand" pictures, showed how a tiny Marine garrison went down fighting after a two-week siege. In many ways it was a model for the war films to come: tough, matter-of-fact fighters

A YANK ON THE BURMA ROAD (1942). With Laraine Day and Stuart Crawford

("Tell 'em to come and get us"); mild American squabbling halted by the attack (Major Brian Donlevy vs. bunkerbuilder Macdonald Carey); appeals to U.S. military heritage (as the invasion barges are sighted an officer shouts: "Don't fire until you see the whites of their eyes!"); bitter battle wit (Robert Preston: "The Japs are blowing us to bits!", William Bendix: "Whad'a you care, it ain't your island!"). Instead of the defeat, we see Bendix and Preston firing defiantly from their foxhole; the smoke of an explosion blots them out, and a grinning Jap runs up and shoots his machine gun down at the two leathernecks. (Americans never surrender!). *Wake Island* was shown at training camps and military installations all over the country, where it was always received enthusiastically, and won an Academy Award nomination as Best Picture. John Farrow was also nominated for his direction.

The British *In Which We Serve*

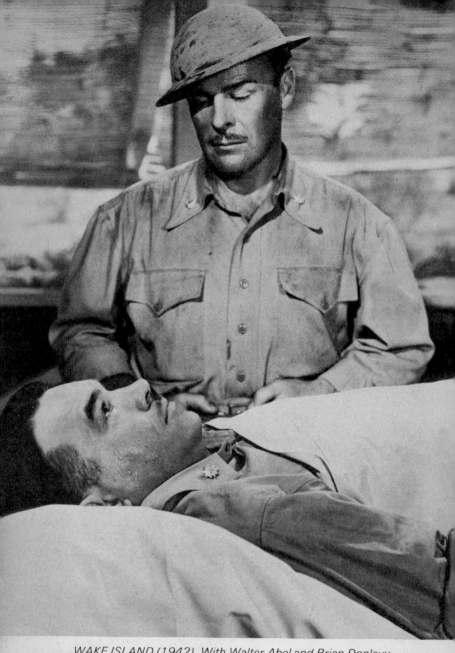

WAKE ISLAND (1942). With Walter Abel and Brian Donlevy

(1942) was a second important early war film. The story of the *HMS Torrin*, from commissioning in 1939 through its defense of the embattled island to its sinking by Nazi dive bombers off Crete in 1941, *In Which We Serve* was written and directed by Noël Coward, who also played the captain. The film was constructed of the memories of survivors as they cling to a lifeboat: the commander remembers a desperate battle in a North Atlantic storm, his home life, and Dunkirk; the seamen and petty officers recall their bombed homes and new children, as well as the terrors of combat. As the *Torrin* goes down, all cheer, further reinforcing the ship's power as a symbol of England's endurance despite adversity. Because the affecting flashbacks occur as the ship is dying, our sympathy and admiration are further increased. Rescued, the captain tells the other survivors: "Now she lies in 1500 fathoms and with her, most of our shipmates. They lie in very good company, with the ship we love. . . . The next time you're in battle, remember the *Torrin!*" The nar-

IN WHICH WE SERVE (1943). With Bernard Miles and John Mills

AIR FORCE (1943). With John Garfield, George Tobias, and Harry Carey

rator concludes: "God bless our ships and all who sail in them!"

An unusual and superior sea story was Lloyd Bacon's *Action in the North Atlantic* (1943), dealing with the lonely work of merchant mariners Humphrey Bogart and Raymond Massey as they drive war supplies across the sub-infested Atlantic to our allies. There are several exciting shootouts between subs and freighters, and the scenes of wounded, weary sailors returning to port, only to join another convoy of "floating firecrackers," gave an idea of the tenacity and patience that is much more important than courage in wartime. A scene with Murmansk Russians cheering: *"Tovarich!"* and Sam Levene explaining: "That means friends!" is often missing from television prints.

An exemplar of World War II films was *Air Force* (1943), the story of the B-17 *Mary Ann* and her crew in the days after Pearl Harbor. Strongly resembling *In Which We Serve*, the film focused on the plane itself and its crew's mutual support. Two important subplots involve sullen gunner John Gar-

BATAAN (1943). With George Murphy and Robert Taylor

field, ready to quit because he couldn't make pilot, and elderly sergeant Harry Carey's concern for his own pilot-son. As the B-17 hedgehops ahead of the Japs from a burning Pearl Harbor (a hospitalized child: "I can't see—why is it so dark?"), across the Pacific (FDR by radio: "The American people will win through!"), to a doomed Wake Island, (Colonel: "We'll teach the Japs that treachery can't win!"), to the smashed Philippines, even Garfield becomes furious: "We're gettin' kicked around all over the place by a lot of stinkin' Nips." Carey learns his son "didn't even get into the air," but at last *Mary Ann* takes on a dozen Zeroes, with a gunner shouting "Fried Jap going down!" Headed for the ground, everyone jumps but Garfield, who, converted, bravely pilots *Mary Ann* in to a crash landing, (a unique No-Man's-Land rescue). On the ground a Zero strafes a drifting crewman parachutist, so Garfield righteously brings him down and even machine-guns the flaming corpse. Repairing *Mary Ann*, the crew takes her off just as Jap invaders swarm into the base, using their rapid-fire weapons to slaughter the enemy. Aloft they spot an invasion flotilla which is joyously sunk by a U.S. airfleet. In the conclusion, the crew is briefed to fly lead bomber on a Tokyo raid: "We're going to play 'The Star Spangled Banner' with two-ton bombs!"

Directed by Howard Hawks, *Air Force* is masterful as a morale-booster, showing such American suffering and fortitude that even Joan Baez would probably be screaming for enemy blood. Although righteous, the film is balanced enough to admit some defeats and limits: Sergeant Carey holding his son's effects: ("Not much to show for twenty years!"); the dumb and resigned old noncoms ("Stick to what you believe in"), the pursuit pilot whom the crew guesses (wrongly) was a coward. *Air Force* does play down U.S. defeats: shattered Pearl Harbor, Wake Island and the Philippines are shown only as smoking runways garnished with wrecked hangars; the actual attacks are limited to flashes of Zeros tearing the glass from control towers; and, in a neat twist, the film keeps our eyes on *Mary Ann* rather than the fall of the Philippines.

Tay Garnett's *Bataan*, the best of

CRY HAVOC (1943). The nurses on Bataan await the enemy.

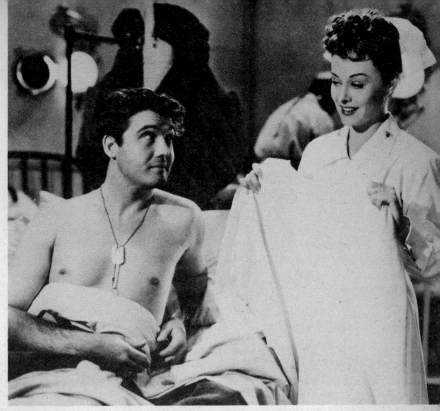

SO PROUDLY WE HAIL (1943). With George Reeves and Paulette Goddard

the last-stand movies, was also made in 1943. *Bataan* told how thirteen soldiers, thrown together, held a bridge against Japan's Philippines offensive. (A squad brought together this quickly could justify including a black American in our nonintegrated services.) A powerful opening revealed the face of the enemy by showing fleeing refugees, civilians screaming as they are strafed by gunfire, and a bandaged blind man staggering amid the bullets. The rest depicted the gradual attrition of the group, slowly picked off except for one who dies of malaria, and mortally wounded pilot George Murphy who dives his TNT-filled plane into the bridge. The inhuman enemy takes on chilling forms in the Pacific, at one point drifting toward them hidden in a milky fog, another time camouflaged into sinisterly shifting trees and brush. In the end, Robert Walker fights the advance back to the edge of his already dug grave, having acknowledged that "It doesn't matter where a man dies so long as he dies for freedom." James Agee has pointed out that the stereotyped characters and foregone deaths make *Bataan* not so much a drama as a kind of native American ritual folk dance—"naive, coarse-grained, primitive, honest, accomplished, and true."*

Two other important last-stand films were *Cry Havoc* and *So Proudly We Hail*, (both 1943), both showing nurses trapped by the advancing Japanese. In *So Proudly We Hail*, Claudette Colbert and Paulette Goddard manage to escape when a bitter Veronica Lake blows herself up with a hand grenade, taking the Japs along. The holding action is given meaning ("It's our present, we're giving them time"), while the monstrousness of the enemy is made clear ("They're machine-gunning! They're strafing the hospital! The beasts! The slimy beasts!"). In *Cry Havoc*, the same ideas are stressed, with tough head nurse Margaret Sullavan announcing: "We're winning the war. That's all that's important." In the end, the trapped nurses surrender, marching out of their bunker with their hands on their heads. What happened next was left to the audience's imagination.

*James Agee, *Agee on Film*. New York: Grosset & Dunlap, 1967, p. 173.

Guadalcanal Diary (1943), based on journalist Richard Tregaskis' book, was close to a last-stand film, showing leathernecks fighting their way through a two month South Pacific offensive, with cabbie William Bendix, wise padre Preston Foster, and tough Sergeant Lloyd Nolan leading the way. Critics praised *Guadalcanal Diary* for the documentary feel of the invasion itself, and as one of the few films which did not use Hollywood motivations (love, bitterness, etc.), but simply had the soldiers driven by the will to stay alive.

As the war expanded, Hollywood had to deal with new locales and stories. *Sahara* (1943), a tribute to Allied determination and courage at El Alemein, was Zoltan Korda's inspired remake of the Russian *The Thirteen* (1937). This time Sergeant Humphrey Bogart, his M-3 tank *Lulubelle*, and some GIs retreating from Tobruk gradually pick up British, French, South African and Sudanese dogfaces, an Italian POW, and after a duel with a Messerschmitt, a German pilot. Because of a strong position at a waterhole, their subsequent wiping out of five hundred swarming Nazis is not too difficult to believe, and effective scripting conveys the feeling of gritty sand and endless heat.

Submarine warfare was also covered in *Crash Dive* and *Destina-*

*GUADALCANAL DIARY (1943). With (left to right) Anthony Quinn,
Ralph Byrd, Richard Conte, William Bendix, Lionel Stander, Reed Hadley,
Richard Jaeckel, and Lloyd Nolan*

SAHARA (1943). With Bruce Bennett and Humphrey Bogart

tion Tokyo. In *Crash Dive* (1943), Hollywood borrowed from pigboat stories like *Hell Below* (1933), that combined a romantic triangle in the conning tower, comedy in the fo'c'sle, and terror in the torpedo room. Lieutenant Tyrone Power, master of ocean demolition, constantly bickers with pigboat skipper Dana Andrews over PT-boats versus U-boats, while they both chase Anne Baxter. The climax makes it worthwhile, however: a spectacular full-color sub wipeout of an enemy sea base, complete with commandos, fuel tanks and ammo dumps going up in colossal pyres, and blazing ships turning turtle. The sub's escape through a sea of burning oil makes the film a pyromaniac's delight!

A second sub thriller, *Destination Tokyo* (1943), sends Captain Cary Grant, the *SS Copperfin,* and her diverse crew to the Aleutians to pick up a weatherman they must place in Tokyo Bay to provide cloud data for Doolittle's raiders. The film might be called "Everything Exciting that Might Happen Aboard a World War II Sub": an enemy air attack, including a bomb wedged into the deck which the skinniest kid aboard must dislodge; an appendectomy performed by the pharmacist's mate; navigating a minefield by following an enemy destroyer; performing the mission, almost in-cidentally; sinking a Jap aircraft carrier; and surviving the greatest depth-charge bombing in history.

Most critics agree that after 1943, our war films became grimmer and less hopeful: too many real casualties and too many newsreels showing the unpoetic facts of combat death made the moviemakers reshape their stories and images. The new harshness showed up in two important films about the air war in the Pacific: *The Purple Heart* and *Thirty Seconds Over Tokyo. The Purple Heart* (1944), based on a real incident, showed the barbarous treatment of American POW airmen, including Dana Andrews, Farley Granger, and Sam Levene. After a bombing raid, eight fliers bail out and land in China, where they are betrayed by a collaborator and illegally put on trial for bombing hospitals and machine-gunning civilians, a sort of publicity stunt to calm the Orientals and scare off future raiders. The filmmakers worked by understatement, never actually showing the atrocities but rather the effects: happy, talkative men broken in spirit, suddenly catatonic, tortured hands in black gloves forever. The airmen's courage and defiant triumph prevent the film from becoming too downbeat.

Thirty Seconds Over Tokyo (1944) reenacted the story of real Doolittle raider Ted Lawson, with

DESTINATION TOKYO (1943). With Cary Grant and Whit Bissell

THE PURPLE HEART (1944). The defiant fliers march to their doom.

Van Johnson as the pilot and Spencer Tracy as his commander. The film follows Johnson from his volunteering and training for a secret mission through a brilliantly filmed sequence of a low-level attack on Tokyo, starting with a carrier takeoff in the middle of a storm to a plunge at zero altitude over ocean and enemy to a crash landing on the China coast. After seeing the pilot's warm, personal life and boundless energy, the amputation of his leg under primitive conditions is all the more tragic and humiliating.

Objective, Burma (1944) had Captain Errol Flynn, fifty paratroopers, and newsman Henry Hull dropped into the jungles to knock

OBJECTIVE, BURMA (1944). Errol Flynn leads the attack.

THIRTY SECONDS OVER TOKYO (1944). With Robert Mitchum and Van Johnson

out a strategic radar station. They succeed, but the troopers are ambushed and miss their pickup, are dogged by the Japs so that they miss a second rendezvous, and must walk out fighting. There are lightning battles with Jap patrols and a butchered village that makes formerly skeptical Hull cry out: "Degenerate immoral idiots! Wipe them off the face of the earth!" The jungle becomes an enemy in its oppressiveness, eerily silent at night except for the screams of strange animals, and finally terrifying as the enemy storms the American camp in the dark. Only a

dozen survive, defending a hill where they've been surrounded, when bomber formations and parachutes pour overhead, signaling the invasion. *Objective, Burma* seems really a last-stand film with a gratuitous happy ending. By contrast, *Back to Bataan* (1945) was flaccid, diluting the combat action with a boy-girl story, a native kid, and a young man proving himself to his warrior ancestors.

Three of the best films about World War II were released shortly after it was over: *The Story of GI Joe*, *They Were Expendable*, and *A Walk In the Sun*. They had much in common: first-rate directors with long experience; sources in superior, intelligent novels and journalism; an understated, episodic, documentary approach to small actions that transformed them into examples of soldierly nobility.

The Story of GI Joe (1945), out of Ernie Pyle's journalism, is William Wellman's beautifully crafted study of a squad of exhausted, dirty, drenched infantrymen, shaped from the style and mood of a documentary, as well as real Signal Corps footage to a much higher and moving perfection. Characters start as almost stereotypes—tough Sergeant Freddie Steele carrying a record of his baby's voice, bragging Italian GI Wally Cassell—but as the film progresses, their behavior, attitudes and subsequent deaths make us understand the exhausting, delirious world of endless combat. Critics noted how the Captain (Robert Mitchum) imperceptibly becomes a towering figure so that his death is a terrible, echoing tragedy. James Agee eulogized the film as "a tragic and eternal work of art" and praised "its ability to build a long, gently rising arch of increasing purity and intensity."* Taut action sequences and comedy are all of a piece with its power, summed up as the men stand exhausted in a shell-torn valley, saying farewell to their dead captain.

*James Agee, *Agee on Film*, New York, Grosset & Dunlap, 1967, p. 173.

THE STORY OF G.I. JOE (1945). The soldiers under attack

THEY WERE EXPENDABLE (1945). With Ward Bond, John Wayne, and Robert Montgomery

They Were Expendable (1945) was John Ford's film of the PT boats that fought a rear-guard struggle in the pullback from the Philippines. Like *GI Joe*, It was episodic, with scenes of the swift little craft, sweeping in to attack enemy battle-wagons, alternating with scenes that stressed the social order, as when an admiral tells Commander Robert Montgomery: "You and I are professionals. If the manager says sacrifice, we lay down the bunt and let somebody else hit the home run." John Wayne has a small romance with Donna Reed, but the emphasis is always on sustaining ritual, as when the crew cheerfully visits a dying officer who murmurs to one who stays behind: "Nice act you boys put on." There is a triumph in General MacArthur's successful evacuation. Even after the last boat is gone, the old boatyard owner waits with his rifle and the sailors as Wayne and Montgomery are ordered out to build a new PT force in the States.

A Walk in the Sun (1945) is also

A WALK IN THE SUN (1945). With Dana Andrews (front)

the story of a small engagement with larger meanings: how a squad captures a Nazi stronghold a short distance from the Salerno beachhead. Directed by Lewis Milestone from Harry Brown's novel, it followed a platoon of American infantry—Sergeant Dana Andrews, Sergeant Lloyd Bridges, Private Richard Conte, and others—as they move toward a final showdown with the enemy, their fears, whims, and hopes expressed in stream-of-consciousness soliloquies as they march along. The story begins when their new lieutenant's face is blasted by a shell; their LST slides up onto the beach; and they move inland. Strafing kills several men and their sergeant cracks from the strain of command, but finally their objective is sighted: a silent farmhouse amid open fields. A patrol crawls toward it but is cut down by machine guns; they try a diversion, then make an hysterical dash for the house. The Nazis spray the plunging troops from their fortress, but at last the survivors close in and toss grenades. The enemy smashed, one GI eats an apple, another notches his gun. The theme comes up:

It's a walk that leads down
through a Philippine town
and it hits highway seven north of
    Rome
It's the same road they had
coming out of Stalingrad
It's the old Lincoln Highway back
    home
It's wherever men fight to be free.

As in 1918, the surrender of the real enemy in 1945 made war movies box-office poison, and it was 1949 before there were any important new releases. From that point through 1957, the films were shaped by the "Korean ambiance," not just the feelings and concerns of that conflict itself, but how it made the Cold War a bloody reality, highlighted and reinterpreted aspects of World War II, and changed the way we looked at our own society. All of these concerns showed up in the important films of this period, notably *The Steel Helmet* (1951).

Samuel Fuller's *The Steel Helmet* was the first important film about Korea. Tough, grizzled Sergeant Gene Evans, survivor of a wiped-out platoon, befriends a Korean boy and then a black corpsman, and at last, grumbling, links up with a patrol headed by insecure Lieutenant Steve Brodie. The battleground is merciless, full of snipers and treachery; when a soldier tries to get a dead man's dogtags, he's blown up by a grenade hidden in the body and Evans laughs at his foolishness. Brodie's patrol, including a mute, a Nisei, a CO corpsman, Evans and the black man, takes refuge in a Buddhist temple, where they capture an enemy POW. The insensitive Americans call South Koreans gooks and the North Korean enemy a Russian. ("I'm not a Russian, I am a North

KOREAN PERSPECTIVES (1949-1956)

Korean Communist.") The captured POW appeals to the minority men, citing U.S. prejudice, but they refuse to help him. Evans treats the Communist like a con artist, and indeed the POW dies asking for last rites as a Buddhist. In the climax the shrine is attacked by endless waves of the enemy. The soldiers rally, with Evans embracing the Buddha in a moment of hysteria. Only Evans, the black corpsman, and the CO survive, grinning crazily. As they move out with the succoring patrol, a title says: "There is no end to this story."

Though the staging of *The Steel Helmet* is inept, the film has enormous emotional force. Evans' furious patriotism, his determination and distrust make his character a driven, half-mad GI Joe; all the characters are crude icons of American beliefs. Race prejudice is handled more honestly than in *Home of the Brave* and other films of the period, but more important, we see a cynical attitude toward *all* beliefs, the director's deep-seated distrust of the new ideals of East *and* West. Fuller struggles to make the Asian conflict feel right by putting it in U.S. terms—Yank confusion as a

THE STEEL HELMET (1951). In front: Steve Brodie. In rear (left to right): Gene Evans, Robert Hutton, Sid Melton, Richard Loo, Richard Monahan, and James Edwards

kind of bigotry, communist ideology as a con game. *The Steel Helmet* is shaped around a great theme of the Korean decade—America's bitter, reluctant taking on of the role of world policeman, in a world now without laws or remorse. The survivors of the platoon—the unkillable sergeant, the militant CO, and the black—have accepted their burden.

Fuller's *Fixed Bayonets* (1951) refined the ideas in *The Steel Helmet*—notably the taking on of leadership in a kill-or-be-killed world: "Somebody's got to be left behind to get their bayonets wet." As the platoon fights a rear-guard Korean action, the leaders are killed off until a sensitive, bookish corporal (Richard Basehart) must take charge. Basehart succeeds. The no-man's-land rescue is mocked as in *The Steel Helmet* when he drags a wounded man back from the middle of a minefield. (Sergeant: "Good

FIXED BAYONETS (1951). With Paul Richards (center) and Richard Basehart (right)

work, Denno, but you were carrying a dead body.")

One Minute to Zero (1952) extended the idea of leadership in a chaotic, brutal world, with Robert Mitchum as a weary U.S. colonel who, in a crisis, orders a band of suspicious North Korean refugee civilians shelled. Luckily, most turn out to be infiltrating enemy troops. Mitchum expresses a bitter defensiveness at our new role: "Nobody's bombed my wife and children —yet." Tough-minded in a way, the film's implicit attitudes of mistrust and race hatred suggest an alternate title: *Fifteen Years to My Lai.*

Several films about Korea used more standard formats. *Retreat, Hell!* (1952) showed the Marines' First Battalion storming Inchon, driving out onto the windy plains where, outnumbered, Colonel Frank Lovejoy cries; "Retreat, hell! We're just advancing in another direction!" and moves his men toward the sea. *The Glory Brigade* (1953) graphically showed battle action even as it pleaded for harmony between U.S. and Greek GIs and UN units, with a climactic rescue from a hilltop siege via helicopter. *Battle Circus* (1953) presaged *M*A*S*H* with Humphrey Bogart as an Army doctor romancing June Allyson between battles. *Cease Fire* (1953) used documentary and on-

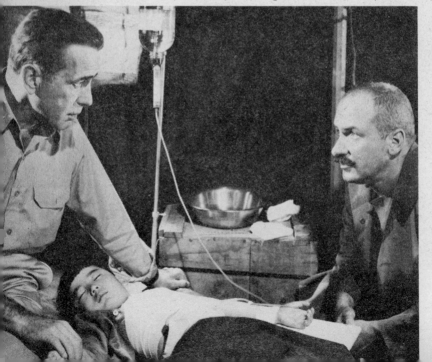

BATTLE CIRCUS (1953). With Humphrey Bogart and Keenan Wynn

THE BRIDGES AT TOKO-RI (1955). With William Holden and Mickey Rooney

TIME LIMIT (1957)
With Richard Basehart
and Richard Widmark

the-spot 3-D footage to reenact a real infantry platoon patrol in a convincing portrait of combat tension. *Men of the Fighting Lady* (1954) told the story of jet pilots launched by carriers in attacks over the peninsula.

The Bridges at Toko-Ri (1955) was a slickly made treatment of the Korean war from the point of view of mature carrier-based Navy flier William Holden, a "retread" family man who justifies the war to his wife in terms of a commissar who will sue for peace when he learns that "they've even knocked out those bridges at Toko-Ri." Otherwise, as in all these films, the war is just men doing their glamorous, dangerous jobs, filmed with the assistance of the U.S. Navy. Most of the best of *The Bridges of Toko-Ri* is pieced together from its immediate antecedents: carrier ready rooms and spectacular catapult takeoffs, bombing runs and mid-air combats, and a climactic helicopter rescue try for a downed Holden by chopper pilot Mickey Rooney, menaced by shadowy North Korean guerrillas. Holden hobnobs with his commander and even the admiral, the way Jimmy Stewart pals around with generals in *Strategic Air Command* (1955), part of a postwar trend toward films about rarefied levels of command virtually unseen before the 1950s.

Several worthy films were made about the soldiers who underwent brain washing. *The Rack* (1956) had Paul Newman as a U.S. Army captain with a wretched Army childhood, on trial for collaboration. Despite his pleas of abnormal loneliness and stress, he is convicted. In *Time Limit* (1957), a sort of defense is made for a sensitive officer, Richard Basehart, who did crack and collaborated after the men in his camp had him execute the stool-pigeon son of a general. In the States the officer, impotent and silent, is finally tricked into revealing the truth. In the end he pleads that there must be a "time limit" to courage. The general forgives neither his son nor the officer. The harsh attitudes toward the breakdowns of soldiers in all these films, despite their sympathetic heroes, point up a new American emphasis on inner toughness even in a hopeless situation. Poor ability, sensitivity, and bad early experiences are no excuse: communists don't play by the rules.

Two early postwar films, *Command Decision* and *Twelve O'Clock High*, showed a new interest in the nature and trials of command. Mixing concern for America's all-powerful new world role with guilt over letting the globe drift into war, these films were, at the same time, allegories of the mental stress of postwar America's "upwardly mobile" society.

COMMAND DECISION (1949). With Clark Gable and John Hodiak

Command Decision (1949) dealt with Air Force General Clark Gable's fight to continue daylight bombing raids despite heavy losses and Pentagon opposition. The film is also fascinating as an exercise in dramatizing the desk-bound commander's burden. Devices include Gable watching takeoffs from his window ("It's all in the kids' hands now"), a talkdown and crash shown only from the control tower, and the general's tortured memories of the sounds of combat as he plans and commands. The film also utilizes a gallery of Capitol Hill grotesques: brass-hat Walter Pidgeon, tight-fisted Congressman Edward Arnold, Pentagon commando Brian Donlevy.

Twelve O'Clock High (1950) told a less complicated story centered on General Gregory Peck driving his men toward "the point of maximum effort" from a nadir of low morale. The film builds well-realized characters who clash with Peck but support him and/or wind up heroes although its best trick is to crank all the tension into one big mission, the ground crews and staff men "sweating it out" as the fortresses fight their way across Europe.

Starting in 1949, another new theme appeared in war movies: racial tolerance. *Home of the Brave* (1949) broke this ground ineptly with black American James Edwards on a recon mission first baited endlessly, then shocked by his best friend's death, with the result that his legs are paralyzed. He's cured by a medic who fires bigoted insults at him so that he stops feeling guilty and realizes he's just like everybody else! ("Sensitivity—that's the disease you've got!") *Go For Broke!* (1951) was a tribute to the Japanese-Americans who fought in Italy; *Red Ball Express* (1952) focused on a ra-

cial incident involving supply truck driver Sidney Poitier; *Between Heaven and Hell* (1956) showed an arrogant Southerner (Robert Wagner) under enemy attack and finally realizing a common humanity with the other soldiers. Stimuli for such films included the budding civil rights movement, wartime inroads and insights into bigotry, and a feeling that the new U.S. world status necessitated better race relations.

Most combat films were not so affected by the new realities. William Wellman's *Battleground* (1949), like his *The Story of GI Joe*, showed a squad of dirty, griping, brave GIs who became the "bat-

TWELVE O'CLOCK HIGH (1950). With Dean Jagger and Gregory Peck

HOME OF THE BRAVE (1949). With Lloyd Bridges, James Edwards, Frank Lovejoy, and Steve Brodie

tered bastards of Bastogne" in the Battle of the Bulge. The emphasis was on plausibility: the snow-covered battleground, the clumsy, heavy-coated dogfaces slogging along or digging foxholes or in a swift, confused firefight with English-speaking Nazi infiltrators (and a near-fight with a stuffy major who can't prove his loyalty with a knowledge of baseball or movies). Van Johnson is likable as a rifleman who drags a dozen eggs through days of combat because he never has time to make an omelet. Very effective too is a chaplain whose field sermon is a simple justification of the war: "Was this trip necessary? Thousands died because they thought it wasn't, till there was nothing left to do but fight. We must never let force impose itself on a free world. Yes, this trip was necessary. Don't let anyone say you were a sucker for fighting in a war against fascism!" But ideas are always in the background. *Battleground* is really most about the look of combat, what Ernie Pyle called "a look that is the display room for what lies beyond it; exhaustion, lack of sleep, tension for too long, weariness that is too great, fear beyond fear, misery to the point of numbness, a look of unsurpassing indifference to anything anybody can do."*

*Ernie Pyle, *Brave Men*, New York, Henry Holt & Co., 1944, p. 90.

Film portraits of World War II combat grew much grimmer and more savage than *Battleground*. *Sands of Iwo Jima* (1949) had a driven John Wayne leading his platoon through bloody skirmishes. *The Halls of Montezuma* (1951) was much fiercer, centering on a bloody murderous island assault. A dying man's comment that "war is too horrible for human beings" is confirmed by Richard Boone's commander on the edge of breakdown, and Lieutenant Richard Widmark's psychotic who must drug himself to be able to fight without rest. *Beachhead* (1954) included several fierce hand-to-hand skirmishes as scouts race through a Jap-infested jungle, and a strong scene in which a whimpering enemy prisoner is given to a helpful murderous native.

Films about special combat forces included two sub stories: *Operation Pacific* and *Submarine Command*. *Operation Pacific* (1951) wasted half its time on John Wayne's pursuit of his ex-wife (Patricia Neal). The rest was action from Warners very much like their *Destination Tokyo:* the ramming of a Jap gunboat; a surfacing amidst the Rising Sun fleet, firing torpedos at random, and a commander who orders a dive though he's trapped on his conning tower. *Submarine Command* (1952) effectively used the last idea for its whole story: the guilt-ridden career of Wil-

BATTLEGROUND (1949). With Richard Jaeckel and Van Johnson

BATTLEGROUND (1949). A pause in the fighting

liam Holden after he had to crash-dive out from under his wounded captain. The well-realized mood and power of the film are spoiled by a triumphant, unbelievable climax. The unusual but enjoyable *Destination Gobi* (1953) showed the adventures of a U.S. Navy weather team in Inner Mongolia.

With the success of *Sergeant York* and *Thirty Seconds Over Tokyo*, filmmakers looked around for more filmic combat biographies. *Above and Beyond* (1952) was a sort of nuclear soap opera, "humanizing" Colonel Paul Tibbets, the pilot

of the Hiroshima strike, by showing how the stress and secrecy of Robert Taylor's assignment led to the blowup of his marriage to Eleanor Parker. *To Hell and Back* (1955), the Audie Murphy story with the war's most decorated GI playing himself, was more successful. It seemed to capture the terrifying fury of combat, the fear and isolation of men face to face with death every day, the desperate resistance of the enemy, and Murphy's incredible, single-handed bravery.

The Korean decade was also the time in which best-selling war

THE HALLS OF MONTEZUMA (1950). With Don Hicks, Richard Widmark, and Jack Webb

novels were bought by Hollywood; they included *From Here to Eternity*, *Battle Cry*, and *The Caine Mutiny*.

From Here to Eternity (1953) was an effective adaptation of James Jones' sweeping novel about soldiers in Hawaii just before Pearl Harbor. One story line is the affair of the popular, tough First Sergeant Burt Lancaster with his superior's wife, Deborah Kerr, carried on even as he holds the unit together with his know-how. Lancaster is a "thirty-year man" who could become an officer and solve his problems, but has only contempt for that caste. Two other important characters are the stubborn, sensitive Private Montgomery Clift, who refuses to box for his company and so receives the "treatment" from the men and the captain, and his amiable friend Frank Sinatra, who can't take degradations masked as discipline, and is des-

ABOVE AND BEYOND (1952). With Robert Taylor and Eleanor Parker

FROM HERE TO ETERNITY (1953). With Burt Lancaster, during the attack on Pearl Harbor

troyed by the sadistic Sergeant "Fatso" (Ernest Borgnine). The climax is the Japanese attack on Pearl Harbor, a vividly photographed scene that shows the terrifying strafing by the enemy planes as Lancaster rallies the men.

Skillfully directed by Fred Zinnemann, *From Here to Eternity* is rich in carefully observed incidents and characters, expressing its ideas without forcing them too emphatically. The point that even good, loyal soldiers are broken and corrupted by the system is made with neither bitterness nor resignation. The Japanese attack negates this in a way, suggesting that whatever went on before the war, things are going to be different now. Pauline Kael has pointed out that Lancaster and Sinatra are 1950s heroes, Lancaster shrewd and unkillable, and Sinatra a "rebel," whereas Montgomery Clift's Prewitt was a real individualist ("If a man don't go his own way, he's nothing"), with his own value system. He is so disturbing in his point of view that his fate was "buried in the commotion of the attack on Pearl Harbor, and it was easy to get the impression that it really didn't matter what happened to him as he would probably have gotten killed anyway."*

The Caine Mutiny (1954) was a "natural" for this period, with its themes of the stress of command and mental illness. The story deals with the gradual breakdown of the *Caine's* captain, Humphrey Bogart, as the ship fights across the Pacific. His collapse is observed by two officers: unhappy but loyal exec Van

*Pauline Kael, *I Lost It At the Movies,* New York, Bantam Books, 1965, p. 43.

Johnson and goading intellectual Fred MacMurray. Striking footage of combat alternates with Captain Bogart's slow but frightening decay: rolling steel balls in his hand; pathetically mouthing clichés; stripping and searching the whole crew to find an extra pantry key; and even running from an invasion beachhead. At the height of a terrifying typhoon, Bogart freezes, and Van Johnson reluctantly takes command. With Johnson on trial for mutiny, sharp lawyer Jose Ferrer badgers Bogart into revealing his madness, but throws champagne in MacMurray's face as the real

THE CAINE MUTINY (1954). With Fred MacMurray, Humphrey Bogart, and Robert Francis

THE DESERT FOX (1951). With William Reynolds and James Mason

mutineer, who spitefully let the situation decay. In the conclusion, the *Caine* gets her old captain back.

The film, beautifully photographed and capably directed by Edward Dmytryk, is exciting because of its cross-purposes. Made with Navy help, the screenplay is stacked to make MacMurray an "intellectual villain," poisoning brave and loyal men who should have supported their battle-fatigued captain. Sometimes it overstates this, as in MacMurray's smug "I'm too smart to be brave!" Yet Bogart, playing against type, dislocates this idea. He is hypnotic as a madman, half-aware of his madness and half a sly, exhausted, desperately unhappy leader. The tensions between the sensible but mundane Navy, the sharp but spiteful intellectual, and Bogart's seductive madness make the film work. In its time it was pointed out as the model of the 1950s conformist executive's dilemma in William H. White's *The Organization Man:* does going along include going down with the ship?

Finally, *Battle Cry* (1955), from the harsh Leon Uris novel, became a mindless melodramatic thriller which followed Marines through boot camp training and fighting across the Pacific basin. The film's big moment has the leathernecks silently fixing bayonets to avenge the death of tough-but-nice Colonel Van Heflin.

One of the unique trends in war movies of the 1950s was the whitewashing of the Nazis from diabolical, genocidal fiends into noble fighters who really hated Der Fuehrer. Early U.S. war films tended to show our ex-enemies as brave and misled (*All Quiet On the Western Front, Hell's Angels*) but were nothing compared to a whitewash like *The Desert Fox* (1951).

The Desert Fox was Field Marshal Erwin Rommel. James Mason played him as the brilliant, determined leader of a handsome, brave Aryan strike force, a master tactician whose genius and daring are all that stand between his little outnumbered army and defeat. He is also a loving family man, wringing our hearts as he says good-bye to wife and children before going to a martyr's death to stop Hitler, when he sees his leader is wrecking the fatherland. The cast of noble Nazis is amazing: Leo G. Carroll as canny Field Marshal Von Rundstedt, Sir Cedric Hardwicke as the Lord Mayor of Stuttgart who sparks the plot, Everett Sloane as a disciplined confederate—aristocrats all; by contrast, Luther Adler's Hitler is a Teutonic Ralph Cramden, a coarse, oafish megalomaniac.

The critical response to *The Desert Fox* was confusion and anger. Nine years after Montgomery des-

THE SEA CHASE (1955). With John Wayne and Lana Turner

troyed the Afrika Korps, we had made a hero of a ruthless enemy who committed treason when his leader seemed to be losing. Today this film can be seen as another view of the 1950s' obsession with command and responsibility in a world of skimpy loyalties, a metaphor of the Cold War. *The Desert Fox*, consciously or not, shows up the issues in *The Steel Helmet* and *The Caine Mutiny:* What *are* the limits of loyalty? What *do* we do when the moral ground shifts under us? Rommel's crisis has become chronic in the Watergate America of the 1970s. *The Desert Fox*, how-

ever, was too much too soon, and in penance 20th Century-Fox produced *The Desert Rats* (1953), a work of huge comic irony in that this pious tale of the heroic Anzacs, with James Mason's Rommel an arrogant, loud-mouthed buffoon, is dull and unconvincing.

The noble Nazi approach was too good to discard. In *The Sea Chase* (1955), John Wayne is an idealistic Prussian sea captain (!) whose rusty freighter is at Sydney, Australia at war's outbreak. Wayne sneaks out of port and heads for the Fatherland "to spit in Hitler's eye," carrying Lana Turner, a Nazi spy, and Lyle

Bettger, a Hitlerite fanatic who pointlessly kills some native fishermen at a fueling stop. In the North Sea after 10,000 miles of dodging the enemy, the freighter meets an English destroyer and engages it. The freighter goes to the bottom but as for Wayne and Turner, by now lovers—"Had the sea taken them, or had they reached the nearby shore, where the fjords could hide a secret?"

Das Teufels General (The Devil's General, 1955) was the German-made story of *Luftwaffe Kommander* Harras (Curt Jurgens), a superbly masculine and compassionate brass-hat and decorated hero. Like USAAF movie commanders of a few years before, he's under pressure from superiors (pal Goering, foe Geobbels), civilian bigwigs (Gestapo men) and contrary subordinates (his aide sabotages Nazi fliers to stop the bloodbath), as well as being sickened by the new government: ("I can't eat as much as I want to vomit"). In the end he takes a bomber up and crashes it when the Gestapo inquisitors close in. The film was based on the true career of German general Ernst Udet.

The Enemy Below (1957) further refined the noble Nazi approach in a destroyer-vs-sub duel; fatigued, ailing and essentially kind Captain Robert Mitchum matching wits with *Unterboatenkommandant* Curt Jurgens, whose two sons have been lost along with his enthusiasm for Der Fuehrer's war. In the climax the destroyer is torpedoed, and the men given five minutes to abandon ship. Mitchum agrees, but rams the sub when it closes in. Picked up by a third vessel, the American and Nazi exchange keen admiration and respect. By this time even the British were doing it—*Pursuit of the Graf Spee* (1957) showed Peter Finch's *Kommandant* Langsdorff almost as heroic as his Anglo-Saxon opposites!

Certainly the climactic war film of the Korean decade was Robert Aldrich's *Attack!* (1956). During the Battle of the Bulge, Captain Eddie Albert breaks his word to supply an advanced squad with reserve troops, and the squad is wiped out. An anguished Lieutenant Jack Palance vows to kill the captain if he lets more die through incompetence, though a lieutenant friend (William Smithers) objects strenuously. In a German counterattack, Albert orders Palance's platoon on patrol, again promising support. The platoon is half-massacred but again Albert won't help. A tattered Palance makes it to the command post where Albert has just cracked up, but in saving a few men nearby Palance is mortally wounded. When a gibbering Albert tries to surrender to the enemy, Palance's friend kills him, the GIs firing into Albert's

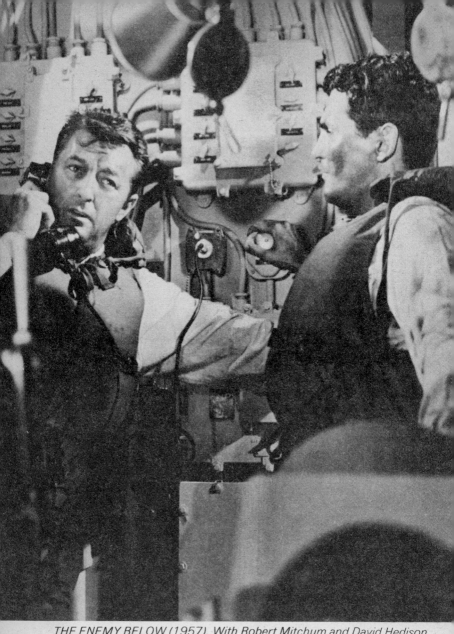

THE ENEMY BELOW (1957). With Robert Mitchum and David Hedison

ATTACK! (1956). With Lee Marvin and Eddie Albert

body as a coverup. But when the friend tells the truth to corrupt Colonel Lee Marvin, whose political ambitions depend on Albert's father, Marvin says he doesn't know what he's talking about. In reply the lieutenant calls their commander, a general, to tell him.

In the history of U.S. war films, *Attack!* is a great watershed: the Cold War themes of the brutality of war, command levels, social responsibility, the nature of the enemy in a shifting moral world are all transformed and transfigured. *Attack!* is the first postwar film to connect the new brutality of war with confusion, corruption, and incompetence of American leadership and American motives—in this sense it is the first Cold War anti-war film. Combat is not just a jungle, it is organized criminal anarchy: a slaughterhouse. Instead of the "nice" Nazis, men like ourselves with bad leaders, *Attack!* shows us the other side of the coin—the criminals, lunatics, and idiots in our own ranks, integrated with the system. The individual's only hope is a private code. The rest is chaos: the captain was a gibbering coward, the colonel is a corrupt opportunist, and as for the general, who knows?

The first important Vietnam war film was Samuel Fuller's prescient *China Gate* (1957). Notably, this was also the time of anti-war films showing how the limits and weaknesses of even a free society could madden and poison its soldiers (*Attack!*, *Paths of Glory*, *The Bridge on the River Kwai*, *The Young Lions*). From these anticipations, the mood and implications of the Vietnam war grew to pervade American filmmaking, as they did most aspects of our national life.

China Gate is made in Fuller's powerful primitive style. It begins with a newsreel showing the Vietnam conflict up to 1954. Angie Dickinson is cast as Lucky Legs, a beautiful halfbreed who married Sergeant Gene Barry and had an Asian-looking child by him—they separated because of it. Now a sort of "Dragon Lady" with northern contacts, she agrees to lead a Foreign Legion patrol to wipe out a VC munitions dump in exchange for her son being brought up in America. The French leader says: "We are fighting for the whole Western World," but no one in the patrol cares: the German soldier simply loves fighting; the black soldier (Nat King Cole) hates the Communists; for Barry it's just a job to finish. Their enemies are just as irrational: tribesmen equally enchanted by posters of Ho Chi Minh

VIETNAM PERSPECTIVES (1957-1973)

or a record of "The Marseillaise;" a junk of murderous sharpshooters; guards instantly bewitched by Lucky Legs. At the bomb dump, the Communist commander, an old flame, makes a play for Dickinson: "Imagine, me a general! Pick the winner!". But Lucky Legs kills him and dies setting off the dump.

China Gate has the same plot as *The Steel Helmet*—an international patrol in which the characters' conflicts are both external and symbolic as they are sent on an almost metaphysical mission. Again, the theme is trying to assimilate a strange new war. At the start, everyone is self-concerned and uninterested: the American Barry considers it a job to finish; Lucky Legs says: "I'd prefer to let you and the hammer-and-sickle boys fight it out alone", the other soldiers are fighting various "private battles." Only at the end, when the job is mixed up with the people they love, does it become a matter of life-and-death. With the reason for fighting gone, Barry takes their child back to the United States. *China Gate* is an anticipation and allegory of the entire Vietnam War and withdrawal, a tragedy of people following their changing feelings to pain, death, and finally understanding.

The combat quickie *A Yank in Vietnam* (1962) was actually filmed there, but is otherwise undistinguished, with a girl-led guerrilla band first rescuing a U.S. major and then her father from the VC. *Commandos in Vietnam* (1965) discreetly left the killing to the Asians, with the American observer only stepping in to save his friends: "We are here at the request of the Vietnamese government." *The Sand Pebbles* (1966) was a Vietnam allegory about a U.S. gunboat caught up in the 1926 Chinese rebellion: "All these people want is to be left alone!" *The Losers* (1970) sent the Hell's Angels to Vietnam on a suicide mission.

In *The Green Berets* (1968) Special Forces Colonel John Wayne (he doubles as director with Ray Kellogg) takes command of a base ("Dodge City") in VC territory. The enemy soldiers are shown as a plague, burning out a village, taking its rice and young men, leaving huddled, soot-blackened women, the tortured chief, and his dead, raped granddaughter. When the base is attacked, a charged fence electrocutes the enemy. Aircraft are called in, and soon enemy bodies are piled high, bright blood on black pajamas.

CHINA GATE (1957). With Angie Dickinson and Gene Barry

THE GREEN BERETS (1968). John Wayne leads the attack.

Even skeptical reporter David Janssen, who had befriended the little dead girl, winds up firing at the VC. Wayne uses a seductive model-patriot as a sex bait dangled before a Communist general, fat with caviar and champagne in a Mekong mansion, roping him out of bed and taking him back to base dangling beneath a 'copter. In the climax Hamchuck, a little orphan boy, is told his Green Beret pal is dead. Wayne gives him the dead man's hat: "You're what this war is all about!" They walk into the sunset. Music: "Ballad of the Green Berets."

The critical response to *The Green Berets* was hysterically negative. *(The New York Times:* "So unspeakable, so stupid, so rotten and false . . . vile and insane!") Aside from liberal biases, it is interesting to see why this film, which uses so many U.S. war movie conventions, was so loathed. Everything is familiar: the defeat-to-victory construction, skeptic-to-believer newsman, hurt child, corrupt enemy, sympathetic GIs. But everything is so overdone that the sewn-together parts become a Frankenstein's monster. Instead of many U.S. defeats followed by a righteous U.S. victory, or at least a last stand *(Air Force, Bataan)*, the savage NFL slaughter of natives is followed by the U.S. electronic extermination of

natives. Instead of a dubious outsider converted by sympathy and facts *(Objective, Burma, Air Force)*, the reporter sees his favorite child killed and grabs a gun. Instead of the suggestion of orphans and child cripples *(Air Force, Bataan)*, one native girl is raped and murdered. Instead of a corrupt enemy bombing hospitals and strafing civilians *(So Proudly We Hail, Bataan)*, the enemy rapes children, swills caviar, and gropes at a slant-eyed playmate. Instead of young idealistic GIs *(Bataan, Air Force)*, the Green Berets are masters of war. (A napalm expert: "My dad gave me a chemistry set, and it just got bigger than both of us".) Fundamentally, American war movies try to justify and make sense of U.S. wars (in *Air Force:* "We'll show the Japs that treachery can't win!"). But *The Green Berets* shows mostly bitterness ("Out here due process is a bullet!"), patronizing defensiveness (to a native child: "You're what this war is all about!"), and a mercenary's fatalism (a Ballad line: "Fighting men, who jump and die!")

The Green Berets had at least crystallized its attitude but earlier, as the sixties approached, war films about the Korean conflict became increasingly vague and ambiguous in their points of view. *Men at War* (1957) continued the theme of the

ALL THE YOUNG MEN (1960). With Sidney Poitier, James Darren, and Alan Ladd

hellishness of battle as a cutoff platoon, under tormented Lieutenant Robert Ryan and instinctive killer Sergeant Aldo Ray is slowly wiped out. *Pork Chop Hill* (1959) used the slaughter theme for heavy irony as Lieutenant Gregory Peck holds a useless hill against endless, faceless Chinese counterattacks, while the peace negotiators bicker. One novel touch is a Red loudspeaker which keeps braying that the attack is pointless, the U.S. deaths useless. Four days after the truce, the hill is made part of the neutral zone, but the legend at the end says: "The Men Who Fought There Know What They Did, and the Meaning of It."

All the Young Men (1960) was one more vague plea for race tolerance,

with Sergeant Sidney Poitier leading a squad of Marines, including sneering "busted" Sergeant Alan Ladd, bigot Paul Richards (his life is short), sweet kid James Darren, American-loving Swede Ingemar Johannson, native American Mario Alcalde, and wisecracking Mort Sahl. *Marines, Let's Go!* (1961) has its stereotyped gyrenes commute between bloody skirmishes and dalliances in Japan with American beauties and Oriental showgirls. The hero of *Sniper's Ridge* (1961) simply wants to go home, and the film shows how he'll do anything to be discharged on the eve of the ceasefire. When his obstreperous captain activates a mine detonator, the GI, papers in hand, sacrifices his life to save him. These odd mu-

SERGEANT RYKER (1968). With Bradford Dillman and Lee Marvin

tant war movies of the early sixties, with their tendencies toward bloodless victories and abstract self-sacrifice, can be seen as disordered products of Kennedy "New Frontier" idealism.

The last, exhausted Korean war films, made in the growing shadows of Vietnam, are heavy with violence, disorder, and self-doubt. *War is Hell* (1964) has a squad sent to destroy a Red bunker but forced to do the job alone, with its cowardly sergeant grabbing sole credit and shooting a dubious superior. Despite the truce, the sergeant then launches a fresh attack and is himself killed in the firefight. An old friend keeps silent, letting the luna-

tic have his medal. *Sergeant Ryker* (1965) is Lee Marvin, captured on enemy ground during what he claimed was a secret mission for his dead commander. He is sentenced to hang for treason, but a new trial only makes his situation worse, as Marvin complains of old U.S. abuses. (The enemy lionized him.) Last-minute evidence of his superior's sneaky system of command saves Marvin.

Films about World War II also continued to be made. Except for the sagas of command, however, these were much less transformed by current events. As critics have pointed out, most Second World War films of the late fifties and six-

THE GUNS OF NAVARONE (1961). With Gia Scala, Anthony Quinn, Stanley Baker, Gregory Peck, David Niven, and James Darren

ties were nostalgic for safer, more ordered conflicts. Thus, *The Naked and the Dead* (1957) reduced Mailer's complex war novel to the furious but derivative story of a doomed patrol of lonely brave stereotypes fighting for a small Pacific atoll. The *Last Blitzkreig* (1959), inverted *Battleground*, with Van Johnson as an English-speaking infiltrator during the Battle of the Bulge who decides he's had enough when a Nazi orders prisoners to be shot down in cold blood.

The Longest Day (1962) was a surging epic of the Normandy invasion, stressing the sacrifice, intelligence and daring involved. The enormous cast and sweeping conflict were well-handled by a group of international directors, though the presence of stars in many key roles was distracting. They included Colonel John Wayne, General Robert Mitchum, Private Red Buttons, General Henry Fonda, Private Sean Connery, General Curt Jurgens, and more. *The Longest Day* covered the entire invasion: Eisenhower's command decision; the Orne River parachute assault; the landing crafts hitting Utah and Omaha Beaches; the British, Canadian, and French Resistance forces at work, as well as the errors and confusion of the German General Staff.

Castle Keep (1967) was an absurd, lovely half-fantasy of combat, with Major Burt Lancaster and some GIs occupying an opulent medieval castle filled with art treasures. The film is long on talky philosophy and eerie humor, but the final stylized battle through the snowy fairyland garden and flaming rococo mansion is magnificently staged.

Films about commandos increased during World War II, but also multiplied in the sixties, suggesting ordinary soldiers were no longer enough (viz. *The Green Berets*). J. Lee Thompson's *The Guns of Navarone* (1961) typified the commando thrillers: a group of hand-picked daredevils—Gregory Peck, Anthony Quinn, David Niven, others—knocking out two giant sea-commanding guns. Action episodes include a climb up a vertical cliff, hand-to-hand combat, betrayals by and executions of partisans, a colossal tidal wave, and the last-minute flaming destruction of the guns. *Tobruk* (1967) was *Navarone* with sand, in which tough Colonel Rock Hudson and fiery Jewish saboteur George Peppard wipe out a Nazi fuel dump, the flaming gasoline burning the sky.

The commando genre itself tended to burn out for lack of new spectacular special effects: *The Devil's Brigade* (1968) was little more than gore and combat clichés (Nazi: "Maybe he can be persvaded . . . ") as the picked men scale a mountainside; *Too Late the*

RUN SILENT, RUN DEEP (1958).
With Clark Gable and Burt Lancaster

Hero (1970) featured an improbable open field across which patrols dash under Japanese fire at the start and end of each mission; *Raid on Rommel* (1971) was reduced to old material from *Tobruk* and Richard Burton for box-office bait.

A group of submarine stories bottomed out in the late fifties. *Run Silent, Run Deep* (1958) was built around the by-now ritual duel of sub and destroyer, with internal conflicts aboard the USS *Nerka* adding tension. (Exec Burt Lancaster wants Captain Clark Gable's job.) Gable, sunk once by the ship called "Bongo Pete," has vowed revenge, and the fearful, stealthy stalk, feint and strike is worked out to the last "Take her down!" and "Fire one!" *Torpedo Run* (1958) used the same tension-laden combat liturgy as Captain Glenn Ford and quarrelsome but loyal exec Ernest Borgnine at last find a Jap carrier in their sights, shielded by a prison transport carrying Ford's wife and child! In the climax the crew gets out with Mommsen lungs, a Hollywood sub routine of the 1930s. Finally, *Up Periscope* (1959) had Captain Edmond O'Brien take the USS *Barracuda* to a South Pacific island so that laconic frogman James Garner can go after a Japanese code book ashore.

The World War II film centering on command rather than combat showed great development during Vietnam (clearing up the "how" in a war where "why" didn't have to be questioned). A fine example of this type was *The Gallant Hours* (1960), a semibiography of Admiral "Bull" Halsey, starring James Cagney, showing no combat but studying the details and ordeals of command. Using techniques partly derived from *Task Force* (1949), *The Gallant Hours* was unusual in dwelling on the actual process of waging modern war. The semidocumentary verisimilitude appears throughout, with Halsey shown as a shrewd, determined, firm leader who tells a panicked flier: "There are no great men, there are only great challenges which ordinary men like you and me are forced by circumstances to meet."

The Longest Day, though a combat epic, too, is also stronger for detailing how the Normandy invasion was carried out, with sharp black-and-white photography adding conviction. *The Battle of the Bulge* (1963), a rip-roaring adventure about the almost calamitous breakthrough in the Ardennes, showed the weaknesses of this approach, shading historical facts with foolish drama, such as the climactic shootout between American GIs and Nazi tiger tanks on a great open snowy plain.

Otto Preminger's *In Harm's Way* (1965) compellingly dramatized the command decisions during the

BATTLE OF THE BULGE (1965). Combat in a French town

post-Pearl Harbor period. After the savage attack, Captain John Wayne is ordered to lead the tiny remaining armada into probable catastrophe, disobeys, and even stops zigzagging to conserve fuel; his ship is badly torpedoed. Reprimanded and reassigned to a desk, he shows top-level talent and is made a rear admiral by sharp CincPac Henry Fonda. Wayne leads Skyhook, the first spearhead against the enemy. The task force does considerable damage before being largely destroyed, but the Japanese retreat in confusion. Preminger not only paints a broad canvas of military men and minds, along with the complexities of running a war, he also links his film to history, taking his title from John Paul Jones' words: "I wish to have no connection with any ship that does not sail fast, for I intend to go in harm's way."

By contrast, *Is Paris Burning?* (1966), the story of the Allies' capture of the French capital, failed as a film because its center—the actions and the characters of leaders—the city's German officials, the Resistance workers, and the U.S. generals—remain mostly obscure. The reason why Hitler's order to burn Paris to the ground was never carried out is hidden; instead the film becomes a mass of dramatic fragments, cameo appearances by stars (Jean-Paul Belmondo, Glenn Ford,

Yves Montand, Kirk Douglas, Simone Signoret), and clumsy dubbing—a disorganized conglomeration without a point of view.

The Bridge at Remagen (1969), was a smaller but more successful command saga, with German Major Robert Vaughn trying to hold the bridge to save his retreating men, as U.S. General E.G. Marshall sends Lieutenant George Segal and Sergeant Ben Gazzara (who scavenges booty from dead Germans), to take it in a raging battle. There is compassion and cruelty on both sides, and ironically, the bridge collapses on its own soon afterward.

Franklin Schaffner's *Patton* (1970) is an epic film centering on George C. Scott's portrayal of the flamboyant, controversial general. We see him first commanding his troops before a gigantic American flag: "Don't just kill the enemy —tear his guts out!" In full-color widescreen images we see Patton commanding a great desert tank battle, leading the Sicily assault (including slapping a shell-shocked GI for cowardice), and watching the massive sweep of his mechanized cavalry through snowy France. *Patton* is not a true command epic (we don't learn enough of the situation and strategy to know whether Scott wins by skill, firepower, or luck), but it is about the audacity and compulsion to command. In it we drink deep of the brew of

IN HARM'S WAY (1965). With John Wayne, Carroll O'Connor, and Kirk Douglas

bravado and cunning. General Scott is a near-megalomaniac, but also electrifying, commanding, and effective. As he brays at the start: "No bastard ever won a war by dying for his country; he won it by making the other poor dumb bastard die for his country." *Patton* lets the viewer really believe and admire this idea for three hours. But the film hints at a second sinister meaning: that it's the Pattons who make us do the dying.

PATTON (1970). With George C. Scott and Karl Malden

A sense of humor starts with a finely developed sense of proportion; comedy, by exquisite exaggeration, makes us laugh by showing when we've gone too far. Bergson sees this as when the gap between body and spirit becomes grotesque; Freud as when we "save our emotional energy" by neatly handling overloaded situations. Both would agree that war and death have enormous comic potential. To the tough-minded, death itself is the body's funniest trick, about which the noble spirit can do nothing. The spirit proclaims: "Ah, I'm going to—" and the dead body keels over like a big dumb animal. "How grotesque!" Bergson would say; "That sums it up!" Freud would comment. Thus war comedies are a fine laboratory for exploring the many species of the comic muse.

Some of the earliest war humor appears in the first over-enthusiastic propaganda films after Wilson's declaration. In *Johanna Enlists* (1918), Mary Pickford is a young romantic whose popularity zooms when a training camp is built next door, to such an extent that she prays, "Oh, Lord, when I asked you for a man, why did you send me a regiment?" Other films showed combat experiences as instantly leveling class barriers, and the flag waving like a magic scarf that ends every social and personal problem—in one film an aphasia

THE COMEDY OF WAR

victim is cured upon seeing Old Glory!

The success of Chaplin's *Shoulder Arms* (1918) produced several war comedies that more carefully parodied the overserious propaganda films of a year or two before. *An International Sneak* (1918) mocked the endless spy stories with Chester Conklin and Ethel Teare as a wacky pair of intelligence operatives; *Yankee Doodle in Berlin* (1919) showed up the hysterical portrayals of the Kaiser's villainy and *Shades of Shakespeare* (1918) was a lampoon of the patriotism-and-preparedness films in general.

But these mocked the familiar war films. The war itself was not taken apart by comic exaggeration until the humorous moments of *The Big Parade* and *What Price Glory?* showed that the fear and pain of the trenches, the chummy squabbling over women and liquor, may have counted for more with the doughboys than the Stars and Stripes.

The undistinguished comedies that followed—*Spuds!* (1927), *Rookies* (1927), *Private Izzy Murphy* (1927), *Behind the Front* (1926)—took the plot of *The Big Parade* but treated it comically all

PRIVATE IZZY MURPHY (1927)
With George Jessel

the way through; they mainly laughed at the "accoutrements" of war and its ancient problems. The typical plot of those films has a clodhopper draftee arriving at a silly training camp, where he meets ferocious sergeants, vain colonels, and even more ineffectual squadmates. He then goes through a slapstick basic, the ill-coordinated body and naive brain betraying the martial aspirations. Sent to France, the dope fights from mock-cesspool trenches against comic-monster Germans, the fiends of the propaganda films now stupefied and swollen by beer and strudel. In a thrilling finale, the bumbling private becomes an impossibly efficient Sergeant York, rounding up dozens of the enemy to become an instant hero, and corralling a U.S. nurse or lovely French girl.

Through the late twenties and thirties, there were few good war comedies. Laurel and Hardy, in *Pack Up Your Troubles* (1932), had slapstick army sequences with the boys dumping garbage into an officer's quarters and Laurel going out to recon No-Man's-Land at midnight in a long flannel nightgown, carrying a candle. But most service films of those years only had comic-relief characters, Jimmy Durante or Jack Oakie, or a few comic sequences with the two heroes outdoing each other to get the girl.

The great exception is *Duck Soup* (1933), the Marx Brothers' magnificent lampoon of nationalism and militarism, and one of the great film comedies. Groucho plays the fast-talking, opportunistic president of "Freedonia," admitting he is a dictatorial, self-interested maniac, and goading the enemy ambassador of "Sylvania" into war out of pure childishness. He suggests the petulent baby inside the purest idealist. When war is declared, flag-waving is mocked in songs like "All God's Chillun Got Guns," and in the antic behavior of Chico and Harpo as inept spies for *both* sides. (Chico finally joins the side with the best chow.) The silly costumes called uniforms are shown up in Groucho's fantastic plumage, and the hidden venal motives behind many a war are noted: "But there must be a war—I've paid a month's rent on the battlefield." The last-minute rescue that saves movie warriors (but not real ones) is exaggerated in a screen filled successively with cavalry, battleships, elephants, bombers, flying fish, and tanks, all rushing to answer Harpo's "Help Wanted" sign.

The preparedness films in the early forties included a few service comedies not much different than those of fifteen years before. Abbott and Costello made *Buck Privates* (1940) and *In the Navy* (1941), simple-minded farces ("The

DUCK SOUP (1933). With the Marx Brothers and Margaret Dumont

MR. ROBERTS (1955). With James Cagney and Henry Fonda

lieutenant says I'm the smartest sailor in the Navy—they can't teach me anything!"), but with a few mild peaks such as Costello in a too-big admiral's uniform commanding a battleship into chaos. Ernst Lubitsch's *To Be or Not To Be* (1942) used Jack Benny as the leader of a theater troop caught in Warsaw during the Nazi invasion, donning the stormtrooper costumes brought along for an anti-Hitler play to sabotage the Reich. Director Lubitsch even let the enemy have a few laughs. Nazi Sig Rumann:

"What you (Benny) just did to Shakespeare, we are doing to Poland." As three decades before, once the war was actually in progress there were no true comedies about soldiering. Instead there were musicals, farces, and fantasies. The peacetime navy was shown in *The Fleet's In* (1942), and World War I jolliness was rampant in *Yankee Doodle Dandy* (1942). Hollywood stars entertained GIs in *Stage Door Canteen* (1943) and *Four Jills in a Jeep* (1944), and training camp was the setting for a red-white-and-blue musical revue in *This Is the Army* (1943).

Again, war movies died at the box office after VJ Day, and, again, the next war comedies followed and were styled on serious war treatments, this time on the cruel, bleak view of combat in pictures like *The Steel Helmet. Up Front* (1951) turned Mauldin's bitter wartime cartoons Willy and Joe into real soldiers, using many of the cartoon's bitter taglines and grubby situations. *Mr. Roberts* (1955) starred Henry Fonda as the decent lieutenant who keeps the SS *Reluctant* on course as she freights supplies around the Pacific, and acts as mediator between fussbudget Captain James Cagney and a crew of juvenile delinquents. When Fonda finally manages a transfer to a fighting carrier, he is killed and Ensign Jack Lemmon takes over the role of gadfly.

One of the most successful and important U.S. war comedies was Billy Wilder's cynical, hilarious *Stalag 17* (1953), with William Holden as a POW camp hustler strictly out for Number One. An introductory sequence sums up the story: men begin a breakout attempt as Holden bets packs of smokes they won't make it; a machine gun fires—and Holden sweeps his new

STALAG 17 (1953). With William Holden, Robert Strauss, and Harvey Lembeck

cigarettes into a foot-locker full of nylons, coffee, and other goods while the men glare. After further frustrations and Holden coups —plus much comic horseplay—the men decide that he must be a stoolie, forcing him to ferret out the real spy. Holden even devises an execution: spilling word of an upcoming escape, then thrusting the agent outside so that he's caught in the searchlight beams from the goon towers, and every gun opens up. In the confusion, Holden himself breaks out.

Stalag 17 derives faintly from the sharpshooting contest in *Shoulder Arms* and more strongly from the money-hungry Marxes in *Duck Soup*: Holden is funny because he is so grotesque—he ignores the war in his money mania so that he seems crazy and contemptible, yet prospers so that he seems to understand the situation best. Besides this, *Stalag 17* has deep roots as a comic allegory of the Korean decade, with Holden as the United States—the hustler nation that grows so successful it must take on the job of world cop—handling it with its own cruel efficiency and righteousness. One should not short the jokes, bits, and comic characters, all skillfully handled by director Billy Wilder, but the themes and ideas in *Stalag 17* powerfully shape U.S. war comedies henceforth—escape, war as business as usual, the reversal of identities (e.g., con man into sheriff).

No Time for Sergeants (1958) is an important comic war movie not for any new ideas but rather as a beautiful refinement of the basic comic "Private's Progress": Andy Griffith, an amiable hillbilly recruit so guileless and obliging he cannot help but cause endless trouble, yet getting exactly what he wants in the end. He's stupid/smart Stan Laurel in khaki, doing everything right and yet wrong, from getting the toilets to salute the inspecting officers to embarrassingly surviving the "fury of the atom" so that he and a pal must be awarded medals in secret and be spirited away to their Shangri-La, infantry school. A comic match is Sergeant Myron McCormick who sums up the fighting peacetime army: "We're a lot of men in canoes—so please stop making waves!".

The Great Escape (1963), *King Rat* (1965), and *Von Ryan's Express* (1965) were all prison camp/escape stories, films elaborate and suspenseful enough to be successful even without humor but laced with mordant comedy, nevertheless. *The Great Escape* involved a breakout by turns grim and high-spirited, the elaborate plan executed with comic ingenuity. Steve McQueen on his getaway motorcycle made an exhilarating figure of fun and freedom. *King Rat*

NO TIME FOR SERGEANTS (1958). With Howard Smith, Nick Adams, Andy Griffith, and Myron McCormick

was a bitter black comedy, a darker version of *Stalag 17*, complete with a prisoner-devised rat racetrack in Singapore's notorious Changi prison, and with "King Rat" (George Segal) surviving by maniacal will and ruthlessness. In *Von Ryan's Express*, Frank Sinatra and British commandos hijack their own prison-train, don Nazi uniforms, and try to "redball" it into Switzerland. It was an enjoyable comic thriller, with everything from a Stuka attack on the speeding train to the mild-mannered German-speaking chaplain forced to become a *Kommandant:* his high-pitched, backward-collar: "I won't do it!" dissolving to a stormtrooper uniform, upraised arm, and "Heil Hitler!"

The Americanization of Emily (1964) was a film made ahead of its time. James Garner, as a scoundrelly admiral's aide (providing fancy food and games), falls for patriotic Englishwoman Julie Andrews. Despite his endless praising of cowardice ("If everybody ran like rabbits, how could we get to the second shot?"), Garner winds up the first man on Omaha Beach, is

VON RYAN'S EXPRESS (1965). With Frank Sinatra and Trevor Howard

reported killed and lionized as a great war hero. He returns, however, none the worse for his experience, and ready to marry Andrews. Like Andy Griffith in *No Time For Sergeants*, he uses comic blackmail, trading on society's hypocrisy to get what he wants. *The Americanization of Emily* is important for experimenting with the basic contradiction of courage and cowardice. Garner is a pontificating version of the heroes of *Catch-22*, hinting at the hidden lunacy which is part of putting on a uniform in the first place.

Robert Aldrich's *The Dirty Dozen* (1967) plunged resolutely into that basic comic madness, with Lee Marvin assigned to train twelve pathologically criminal GIs — psychopath John Cassavetes, degenerate Telly Savalas, murderer Charles Bronson, white-hating Jim Brown, and others — for the suicide mission of wiping out a Nazi officers' resort in occupied France, the survivors to be pardoned. Major Marvin reacts: "Whoever dreamed up this scheme must have been a lunatic!" But he ruthlessly trains his maniacs, who are the ultimate in stereotyped, truculent GIs. English war games show what the men can do: hooligans in khaki, they swap sides as needed, kidnap referees, hijack an ambulance, and capture the enemy command post seemingly seconds after "war" is de-

clared. In the exploding, bloody Keystone Kops climax, the Dozen use the same ruses and ruthlessness to reach the chateau, savagely wiping out the enemy brass by turning the elegant building into a flaming deathtrap. Three less-than-hopeless men, along with Lee Marvin, survive.

Critics at the time were mostly shocked and revolted by *The Dirty Dozen*, seeing it as the glorification of killing and sadism, morbid and disgusting. On the same limited literal level, most "Tweety and Sylvester" cartoons are serious indoctrination in the joy of torture and inflicted pain. For *The Dirty Dozen* are cartoons too, comic monsters, outrageously funny because they are commandoes *all the time* — savages with fangs and claws and fur showing, the monsters we need during wartime to kill, but upsettingly hanging around. The *Dirty Dozen* goes to the basic contradictions of war for its acerbic humor, mocking us with the killer instinct society endlessly works to leash but can't do without. It also shows the other side of that instinct, the wish to be controlled and doomed — the rotten GIs barely hidden savoring of their hopeless assignment, testing and then submitting to Lee Marvin, leader on their suicidal job. (Nobody talks about "When I get back—.") Yet the film does not despair of society;

THE AMERICANIZATION OF EMILY (1964). With Julie Andrews and James Garner

rather, Marvin and the men go back to the start and build it again, so by the time they jump they are a loyal tribe of their own, making war no more savagely than the allies. *The Dirty Dozen* plays humorously with ideas to show war's grotesqueness in a way which has been refined, but not surpassed.

The two most recent first-rate war comedies were Mike Nichols' *Catch-22* (1970) and Robert Altman's *M*A*S*H* (1970). In some ways they are mirror-images, *Catch-22* about fliers exploded into separate manias by the insane society of war, *M*A*S*H* about soldiers maintaining style and community in the midst of war's inferno. Like *The Dirty Dozen*, both detour past individual and social humor to pathology and anthropology as wit.

As B-26s roar off to hit Italy, *Catch-22*'s bombardier Alan Arkin makes a "deal" with obnoxious colonels Martin Balsam and Buck Henry: instead of causing trouble, he will praise them at bond rallies at home. Alone, Arkin dreams how he tried to help a wounded flier but found him eviscerated, the plane's first-aid kit stripped by a lunatic corporation. In scrambled incidents we see Arkin's society: Balsam whose dream is to be written up in the *Saturday Evening Post*; General Orson Welles, whose favorite command is: "Take him out and shoot him!"; Mess Officer Jon Voight who turns the war into a money-making business that even sends U.S. planes to bomb their own field; the pleasant whorehouse sacked by MPs who chant: "We can do whatever you can't stop us from doing!" Insanity is no way out; "Catch-22" says: If you say you're crazy, you're not. Waking in the hospital, Arkin reneges on his deal with the colonels and deserts, headed for Sweden.

Catch-22 is about men driven mad by a society gone crazy; half *The Dirty Dozen*, half *Duck Soup*. As in *Duck Soup*, respected leaders become demented babies who shoot people for a whim, or lust to be seen on magazine covers, make mountains of money, or impress moronic superiors. Laws and justice are reduced to "anything you can't stop me from doing!" Like *The Dirty Dozen* the fliers are idiots or maniacs. One is so shy he is catatonic; another gets tired of a whore, so he simply flings her out a third-floor window; the celibate squad moans hopelessly at a pinup nurse. The mood of *Catch-22* is very uneven and many of its actors have no talent for comedy, but this is an important war comedy. Its hard-to-spot moral is that modern society makes war particularly dangerous because its goals and meanings are swiftly lost in absurd social rituals and lunatic obsessions.

THE DIRTY DOZEN (1967)
With Lee Marvin and Clint Walker

CATCH-22 (1970). With (left to right) Martin Balsam, Richard Benjamin, Orson Welles, Austin Pendleton, and Buck Henry

M*A*S*H* begins with two 'copters, carrying wounded on stretchers, flying through Korean valleys to land at a mobile army surgical hospital. "Hawkeye" Donald Sutherland and "Trapper John" Elliott Gould are surgeons whose operating alternates with hip horseplay: humiliating beautiful but priggish nurse "Hot Lips" Sally Kellerman by dropping her shower tent and bugging her lovemaking (the loudspeaker roars: "I got hot lips —kiss my hot lips!"); salvaging a sexually insecure dentist from suicide with promiscuous Lieutenant Dish; blackmailing an Army hospital head so they might operate on the sick baby of a Japanese whore; and finally winning a football game by drugging the opposition's captain while even "Hot Lips" cheers.

M*A*S*H is the obverse of *Catch-22*, full of jokes and wit, but fundamentally about a happy, lively, sane society in the middle of meaningless war. In a way, Korea is irrelevant, but redone as a *Crazy Hospital USA*, the film would lose

M*A*S*H* (1970). With Donald Sutherland

its necessary contrast with the slaughter going on outside, for this society is virtually painless. The only discipline is that people do their jobs well. "Hawkeye" and "Trapper John" are comic medicine men, initiating Sally Kellerman to the tribe, restoring a brave's potency, helping a pariah, hustling a symbolic tribal victory. These comic shamans make us laugh by how clearly they see how a society should work, and the neat, swift way they set things right, so much better than our own institutions. An untelegraphed effect is the comforting work of the $M*A*S*H$ unit itself: the answer to all those frustrated, doomed No-Man's-Land rescues: airborne evacuation to first-rate surgery.

The special American challenge to arguing against war would seem to be: "Well, so long as you've got to fight, winning is better." The history of the anti-war film is a series of responses to this statement.

Many of the first anti-war films were simple fables, sermons, and wish fulfillments. In *War o' Dreams* (1915), a young man invents a kind of A-bomb, which later kills thousands in an American adventure; guilty, he commits suicide with his formula—but all this turns out to be his dream (a subtle appeal until you recall that it was Einstein who wrote to Roosevelt). *One Of Millions* (1914) had a war widow driven mad by seeing her husband's uniformed corpse. *War Brides* (1916) was "Lysistrata updated"; when a king of a Teutonic nation announces all singles must marry to manufacture more cannon-fodder, a peasant wife whose husband and sons are war dead demonstrates against him, finally killing herself in protest.

Two anti-war films important in early film history are Thomas H. Ince's *Civilization* (1916) and D.W. Griffith's *Intolerance* (1916). Eileen Bowser has pointed out Ince's sly calculation in *Civilization:* for preparedness fans an evil warlord, slaughter, starving civilians: for the millions who wanted peace the "miracle of divine intervention or the equally miraculous uprising of

ANTI-WAR FILMS

the mothers of the race,"* with Christ in a war hero's body and battalions of Lysistratas finally stopping the military-industrial complex. Griffith's *Intolerance*, a landmark in film history, showed his pacifist feelings clearly, but was more truly about the meaner emotions themselves: hate, envy, cruelty, intolerance itself, and how they drive history.

As war became more likely, the supply of anti-war films dried up and then was cut off by government decree. Instead, films like *The Battle Cry of Peace* (1915) showed the Huns as a gang of Specks, Mansons, and Scorpios. Pacifists were depicted as numbskulls and traitors: in *A Nation's Peril* (1916), a female pacifist turned patriot sees the light and winds up herding men into the recruiting office; *In Again, Out Again* (1917) has peace protesters making millions on the sly by selling munitions to the Kaiser; *The Fall of a Nation* (1917) attacked pacifist priests and national anti-war figures including William Jennings Bryan, its protagonist a politician who dis-

*Eileen Bowser, *Film Notes*, Museum of Modern Art, New York, 1969

128

INTOLERANCE (1916). The Babylon sequence

ALL QUIET ON THE WESTERN FRONT (1930). With Ben Alexander and Lew Ayres

arms America so it is easily overrun by Teutonic invaders.

Plays with anti-war themes were watered down by the time they reached the screen. *What Price Glory?* (1926), despite dying mama's-boy Barry Norton's screams of "Stop the blood! Stop the blood!" was nailed by Eileen Bowser: "The film pays lip service to the 'war is hell' sentiments, but defeats them by putting them in the mouths of weaklings who get killed while military careerists lament 'civilians' being in the war at all."* *Journey's End* (1930) was a more serious work,

*Eileen Bowser, *Film Notes,* Museum of Modern Art, New York, 1965.

showing how the war eroded and brutalized even superior individuals forced to endure it for years.

The strongest anti-war statement of this period was *All Quiet On the Western Front* (1930), based on Erich Maria Remarque's worldwide best-seller. It focuses on Paul (Lew Ayres), a German schoolboy who is taught that war is noble and service to the Fatherland is all. He volunteers for brutal training and is initiated into the horror of combat in a midnight wire-stringing that ends in shots, screams, and a sergeant cursing a would-be rescuer: "It's just a corpse, no matter whose it is." The next day Paul runs berserk in

ALL QUIET ON THE WESTERN FRONT (1930). With Louis Wolheim and Lew Ayres

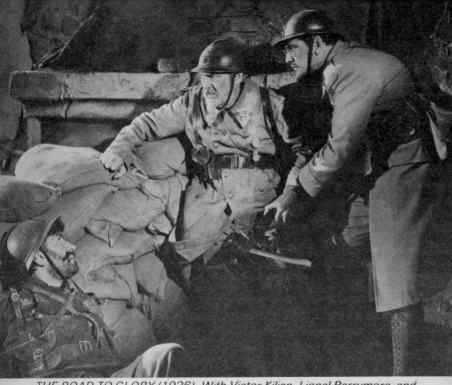

THE ROAD TO GLORY (1936). With Victor Kilian, Lionel Barrymore, and Fredric March

the trenches, and from then on war is shown as a death machine: hand-to-hand trench battles with fixed bayonets, hysterical counterattacks, a hospital "death room" from which no casualty returns. In No-Man's-Land Paul kills a Frenchman, then listens all night while he dies in agony. Paul and a French girl make (offscreen) love, but next day he marches past stacks of coffins. Sent home, he finds his teacher still mouthing lies; returning to the front, he finds his friends mostly lost, and even the battle-wise Sergeant Katz machine-gunned by a Spad. In the last scene, a brief lull, Paul reaches over the parapet for a flower; a sniper fires, and Paul's fingers go slack. In the epilogue, a ghostly line of soldiers march into a void, their eyes bitter.

The film denies any meaning to the last war, showing a soldier as a terrified, humiliated statistic fighting for his life by somebody else's rules. It also suggests that his government really makes little difference: when young, he is conditioned so deeply by family and school that he can never break free. The film was an international success: Nazis had to release snakes and rats in theaters to drive out audiences; Hitler banned it outright. Only a heavily cut version was shown during the Korean War, and it could not be shown in France until 1962.

All Quiet On the Western Front was the first of many anti-war dramas through the 1930s. G.W. Pabst's *Westfront 1918* (1930) showed a German unit holding the line at suicidal cost, with one soldier finding his wife has betrayed him for extra meat. Ernst Lubitsch's *The Man I Killed* (1932) dealt with a French soldier who seeks out the family of a man he killed in combat, the man he dreams of every night. Much of it is sentimental, but strong satire includes scenes of soldiers in a church, scabbarded swords lining the aisles, kneeling to pray so we see their spurred boots. *Neimandsland (No-Man's-Land*, (1932) shows five soldiers of different nations caught in a shell hole learning to work together for survival, an anticipation of the ethnically assorted squads and crews of Hollywood's World War II. *Les Croix de Bois (Wooden Crosses*, 1932) followed an *economic* cross-section of France —an intellectual, a small-businessman, farmers, some workers—into combat, again ending with the ghostlike casualties marching, Christlike, with wooden gravemarkers over their shoulders. John Ford's maudlin *Pilgrimage* (1933) continued this cortege, with a Gold Star mother visiting her son's grave in France; somehow this makes her accept the boy's bastard son and his mother.

Howard Hawks' *The Road to Glory* (1936) showed French draftees, including a pathetically ancient retread from the Prussian seige of 1870, ordered to hold their position by opportunist-officers even as they hear Germans tunneling to mine it. *The Road Back* (1937) indicated how badly the subject had frazzled. The Remarque novel, depicting young German veterans' frustration and loss, was a serious, bitter work. But on film the excruciating journey home involves slapstick revels in a tavern, and the vicious street gangs who beat the veterans are cowards frightened by an apple swung like a grenade. Clichés like ghostly figures taking over the ranks of the mustered-out-men, and an old schoolmaster spouting prewar platitudes, are trotted out shamelessly.

Two significant works in film history were also the last expressions of pacifist feelings before World War II: Jean Renoir's *La Grandè Illusion (Grand Illusion*, 1937), and Charlie Chaplin's *The Great Dictator* (1940).

Grand Illusion begins with

*LA GRANDE ILLUSION
(GRAND ILLUSION) (1937).
With Erich von Stroheim*

downed French officer airmen toasted by their German counterparts. Soon they are moved to a prison camp full of fraternizing Allied soldiers, but a French captain (Pierre Fresnay) finds more camaradierie with his fellow decadent aristocrat, the camp commandant (Erich von Stroheim). When the French officer leads a diversion during an escape attempt, however, the commandant coolly shoots him down. The two privates who do escape can only bicker; one is a vicious anti-Semite, eventually sheltered by a German war widow, who sleeps with him. Headed for Switzerland, the Jew-hater exclaims: "Nature all looks alike. Frontiers are an invention of man!" At the border, a patrol has both men in their sights—but doesn't fire. They cross the imaginary line into Switzerland.

Most critics see *Grand Illusion* as a metaphor for the transformation of European society after the First World War—the French are fighting the Germans, but self-destructive aristocrats (officers) of both sides really have a great deal in common, as do the new bourgeois and working classes (prisoners, guards). Thus the war is a mistake, a great illusion that brings destruction and self-torment to those who believe in it—Fresnay and von Stroheim—but lets the people who see through it—the escapees, the German widow—achieve pleasure and freedom. The climax suggests the fantastic nature of the war—the patrol that doesn't fire after the two privates cross the border, an imaginary line. One must admit that Renoir's concern with the gentlemanly wars of the past makes his elegant film of limited relevance to today's furious struggles with their violently clashing ideologies.

Chaplin's *The Great Dictator* is a great comedy, a powerful anti-war film, and a twentieth-century work of art. Charlie, as a little German Jewish barber, is injured and suffers amnesia in World War I. Back in the ghetto, he does not notice the roving bands of Jew-baiters, and the new double-cross emblem everywhere. He is especially unaware that the megalomaniacal dictator Hynkel is his double. Chaplin's mocking of Hitler offered the most inspired moments in the film: the weak, affected heils, the manic-depressive fits of weeping and rage, the grimacing and posturing, the bulging eyes. Beautiful set pieces include Hynkel's famous ballet with a giant balloon marked like a globe (an eerie yet hilarious expression of the monster's ambitions for world conquest); Hynkel's scene in a barber shop with ally Benzini Napaloni (Jack Oakie), showing the childish egomania of dictators as the two throttle their chairs skyward in an absurd race for status. Hitler's

THE GREAT DICTATOR (1940). With Paulette Goddard and Charlie Chaplin

THE GREAT DICTATOR (1940). With Reginald Gardiner and
Charlie Chaplin

mania for magic weapons and indifference to human life are shown with a man who says he's invented a parachute hat—Hynkel orders him out the window, and as he watches we see his head twist abruptly downward. "Please don't waste my time with these things until they are perfected," he murmurs to his minister of war. At the end of the two-hour film, the fleeing barber, mistaken for Hynkel, comes abruptly out of character to deliver a long, passionate protest, completely serious, against the Nazis:

"In the name of democracy, let us unite."

The Great Dictator was generally praised as a sincere attempt to stem the tides of war. Only Chaplin's "straight" ending was criticized as adding a jarring note to a comic film, to which he replied: "May I not be excused for ending my comedy on a note that reflects honestly and realistically the world in which we live, and may I not be excused in pleading for a better world?" The critics interpreted his long plea in different ways: Bosley Crowther in

THE BRIDGE ON THE RIVER KWAI (1957). With Sessue Hayakawa and Alec Guinness

The New York Times called it "an appeal for reason and kindness"; film scholar Lewis Jacobs thought of it as a call for immediate aid to embattled Britain.* In any case, the film is a triumph, a film genius' sincere attempt to avert World War II.

There were few anti-war films until the late fifties, but three films of that period were powerful anti-war statements. David Lean's

The Bridge on the River Kwai (1957) shows a Japanese officer (Sessue Hayakawa) and a British colonel POW (Alec Guinness) in a Japanese labor camp, learning to admire and respect each other as they build a strategic bridge that becomes, for the colonel, a labor of love. In the tragic ending, the blindly heroic, obsessed colonel tries to stop the commandos sent to blow up his triumph. With everyone machine-gunned and the beautiful bridge in ruins, a character cries: "Madness, madness!"

*Lewis Jacobs, "World War II and the American Film," *Cinema Journal*, Vol. III, Winter, 1967-68, pp. 21-22.

PATHS OF GLORY (1957)
With Kirk Douglas

THE VICTORS (1963). With George Hamilton, Vincent Edwards, James Mitchum, and George Peppard

Stanley Kubrick's *Paths of Glory* (1957), based on true events, has no enemy at all, dividing the French forces in World War I into battered, blood-soaked soldiers and a ruthless, ambitious officer corps controlled by a ruthless general (Adolphe Menjou). When a murderous attack fails, three innocent privates are tried for "cowardice" and shot to placate the press and high command. A liberal officer (Kirk Douglas) who stands up for them is treated with contempt by his superiors, and the war itself grinds on. (*Paths of Glory* is still banned in France).

Perhaps the best of these films was Edward Dmytryk's *The Young Lions* (1958), which, like the other two, demonstrated how social systems and class conditioning, destructive in peacetime, become deadly madness in war. René Jordan writes perceptively: "(Marlon Brando's German is) a social climber who dons the olive green of Hitler's army to get ahead in a stratified society . . . a go-getter doomed from the word go."* In other scenes, Montgomery Clift, a young American Jew enlisting to help close down the gas chambers, is tormented by anti-Semites in his own ranks.

The idea that war is a catalyst which brought out the worst in people, not a system that made monstrous behavior necessary, was advanced in several sincere but weak pacifist films in the early 1960s. The ambivalent but interesting *The War Lover* (1962) was about Buzz Rickson (Steve McQueen), a flyer who delights in his B-29 bombing raids. His copilot's girl attacks his point of view, claiming that the real reason for war is that some men enjoy it—"not just the campaigns, getting away from responsibilities, not taking care of others, but the dark, slimy places, deep down" (a darkness celebrated in *The Dirty Dozen.*) But the film ends with Rickson dying heroically, trying to solo his crippled bomber back to England. The heavy-handed *The Victors* (1963) was a panorama of personal "ugliness" triggered by war: shameless beauties who shack up with GIs for food and kicks; a dog-mascot shot for target practice; the execution of a deserter on Christmas Eve (!) while Frank Sinatra croons "Have

*René Jordan, *Marlon Brando*, New York, Pyramid Publications, 1973, p. 83.

Yourself a Merry Little Christmas," all intercut with newsreels of homefront foolishness.

The mid-sixties were notable for several very successful and exciting films criticizing the Cold War's "balance of terror." Certainly the most perceptive and amusing was Stanley Kubrick's *Dr. Strangelove* (1964), about a psychotic general (Sterling Hayden) who orders the nuclear bombers to attack Russia, and the desperate attempts of the desperate president (Peter Sellers) to stop the B-52s before they can trigger the Russian Doomsday Device, a machine which ensures peace by guaranteeing to end all life on earth, the ultimate Cold War paradox. The film was enriched by witty dialogue and beautifully satirized American types, including a bungling and aggressive Pentagon general (George C. Scott) and an unstoppable Texas pilot (Slim Pickens) who ultimately rides the bomb, like a broncho, to its target. Peter Sellers also played two other roles: the baffled British officer, Captain Mandrake and Dr. Strangelove himself, a maniacal German scientist who cannot restrain his arm from giving the Nazi salute. Critic John Simon detailed the antiwar implications of the film: "There are no rebels, only heroes: heroes of politics, warfare, science, all of them so repellent, or at best nondescript, that the only rebels

DR. STRANGELOVE (1964). With George C. Scott, Peter Bull, and Peter Sellers

must be in the audience."* One important source of humor was a shrewd mocking of the clichés of war movies: the ethnic mix of the B-52 crew, the ferocious, absurdly pious commanders (who are also insane), and most of all the inversion of our feelings, so that we cheer on the bomber even though success means annihilation.

Two other films on this topic were *Fail Safe* (1964) and *The Bedford Incident* (1965), both handling the problem seriously. *Fail Safe* had the *Strangelove* plot, with President Henry Fonda trying to stop an accidental "first strike," and when the plane gets through, ordering New York City bombed to repay the destruction of Moscow. *The Bedford Incident* was an encounter between an American destroyer and a Russian sub that escalates into nuclear catastrophe (the ultimate destroyer vs. U-boat suspense film). With their intellectual/action format, all three films are superior to the dreary "stiff-upper-lip" fallout-opera *On the Beach* (1959).

How I Won the War (1967), written by Charles Wood and directed by Richard Lester, is a special example of the anti-war film: an attempt to use jokes, genre clichés, and surrealism to show the evils of war. We follow a World War II platoon run by incompetent Lieutenant Goodbody (Michael Crawford)

*John Simon, *Private Screenings,* New York: Macmillan, 1967, p. 92.

whose men, comic boobs, are nevertheless slaughtered or go crazy on idiotic missions. They are replaced by ghosts tinted to match the "bubble-gum cards" that introduce each battle—symbolic of how little they meant. Goodbody is captured, finds his suave Nazi keeper "the first person I can really talk to" though he has killed "quite a lot" of Jews, and buys a Rhine bridge for a ventriloquist Eisenhower whose dummy Churchill chants "I want a battle!" from his lap.

The film was a popular and critical failure, reviewers arguing that Wood chose the "wrong" war, one with real moral justification, and aimed at outmoded targets such as class snobbery.

Oh! What a Lovely War (1969) continued a trend to comic outrage and "distancing." World War I becomes a cheerful spectacle set on a Brighton amusement pier: pop songs, sexy girls, flashing signs. A giant scoreboard counts the dead, strategists bicker, men push surrealistically through turnstiles to the trenches. The finale shows the last day, score nine million. A soldier follows a red tape maze through

HOW I WON THE WAR (1967). With Roy Kinnear and John Lennon

OH! WHAT A LOVELY WAR (1969). With John Mills

smoke, peace talks, patches of poppies. His family picnics on a hill, and the camera pulls back to show thousands of grave markers. Critics argued that making folly of a long-ago war was an exercise in righteousness, pointing out that this film made war simply an upper-class idiocy.

Masterfully photographed and acted, Ingmar Bergman's *Shame* (*Skammen*, 1968) is the most powerful film statement of what war means today. It starts in a mythical 1971, as the Rosenbergs (Liv Ullman, Max von Sydow), once violinists, flee to an island to escape a European civil war. Exempt and indifferent, the couple farm and play. When the conflict spreads, they are arrested and interrogated, and a film of this is used for propaganda. A defense colonel gets them released, but sleeps with the wife, so that when guerrillas capture all three, the husband bitterly shoots him. Their home destroyed, the couple flee in a small boat. As the boat drifts, lost, they see shoals of dead soldiers in the water.

On one level, *Shame* depicts modern war as a senseless, destructive force, wiping out homes and lives and societies in lightning raids and spectacular conflagrations. The ideologies behind it are obscure or meaningless, yet it is practiced with all the "means" of modern society, so that torture is allowed and any position is grist for the propaganda mill. In opposing war, only the primal drive to survive might be trusted, even as it brutalizes other feelings and beliefs. It has been pointed out that Jan (Von Sydow) resembles the contemptible intellectuals who "adjusted" to the Nazis, and to Vietnam. Finally, the film seems to suggest the peculiar Swedish shame of non-involvement in past wars, showing how it leads to ruin.

With the (temporary?) winding down of the war in Southeast Asia, there has been a lull in the anti-war genre. Movies like the delightful *FTA* (*Free The Army*, 1972), showing Jane Fonda and other radical entertainers on a stop-the-war-soldier tour of the Pacific Basin, and other films with our disillusioned Viet Vets using counter-insurgency tactics against various stateside enemies, suggest new directions for the anti-war film.

SHAME (1968). With Liv Ullman and Max von Sydow

BIBLIOGRAPHY

Agee, James. *Agee on Film.* New York: Grosset & Dunlap, 1967.

Alloway, Larry. *Violent America: The Movies 1946-1964.* New York: Museum of Modern Art, 1971.

Baxter, John. *The Cinema of John Ford.* New York: A.S. Barnes & Co., 1971.

Bowser, Eileen. *Film Notes.* New York: Museum of Modern Art, 1969.

Browne, Michael. *Survey of the Hollywood Entertainment Film During the War Years, 1941-1943.* M.S. thesis, U.C.L.A., 1951.

Farber, Manny. "Movies in Wartime," *National Review*, January 3, 1944.

Furhammer, Leif and Folke, Isaksoon. *Politics and Film.* New York: Praeger, 1971.

Hardy, Phil. *Samuel Fuller.* New York: Praeger, 1970.

Higham, Charles and Greenberg, Sam. *Hollywood in the Forties.* New York: A.S. Barnes, 1968.

Hughes, Robert, ed. *Film: Book 2: Films of Peace and War.* New York: Grove Press, 1962.

Jacobs, Lewis. "World War II and American Film," *Cinema Journal*, Vol. II, Winter 1967-68.

Jones, D.B. "Hollywood Goes to War," *The Nation*, January 27, 1945.

Jones, K.D. and McLure, A.F. *Hollywood at War.* New York: A.S. Barns, 1972.

Kagan, Norman. *The Cinema of Stanley Kubrick.* New York: Holt, Rinehart & Winston, 1972.

Kreuger, Eric. "Robert Aldrich's *Attack!*", *Journal of Popular Film*, Summer, 1973.

Lingeman, R.R. *"Don't You Know There's A War On?"* New York: G.P. Putnam's Sons, 1970.

Morella, Joe, Epstein, E.Z. and Griggs, J. *The Films of World War II.* New York: Citadel Press, 1972.

Sauberli, H.A. *Hollywood and World War II: A Survey of Hollywood Films About the War.* M.A. thesis. U.C.L.A., 1967.

Spears, Jack. *Hollywood: The Golden Era.* New York: Castle Books, 1972.

Stern, Seymour. "The Birth of a Nation," *Film Culture*, Spring-Summer, 1965.

Wanger, W. "Movies with a Message," *Saturday Review*, March 7, 1942.

Wood, Robin, *Howard Hawks.* New York: Doubleday & Co., 1968.

FILMOGRAPHY: THE WAR FILM

Because of the large number of significant war films, this chronological listing is very selective, and is limited to those films of great popular and critical success.

The director's name follows the release date. A (c) following the release date indicates the film was in color. Sp indicates screenplay and b/o indicates based/on.

THE BIRTH OF A NATION. Epoch Producing Corp., 1915. *D.W. Griffith.* Sp: D.W. Griffith and Frank E. Woods, b/o novel and play *The Clansman* and *The Leopard's Skin*, all by Thomas Dixon. Cast: Lillian Gish, Mae Marsh, Henry B. Walthall.

SHOULDER ARMS. First National Release, 1918. *Charles Chaplin.* Sp: Charles Chaplin. Cast: Charles Chaplin, Sydney Chaplin, Edna Purviance.

THE BIG PARADE. MGM, 1925. *King Vidor.* Sp: King Vidor, b/o story by Laurence Stallings. Cast: John Gilbert, Renée Adorée, Tom O'Brien, Karl Dane.

WHAT PRICE GLORY?. Fox Film Corp., 1926. *Raoul Walsh.* Sp: James T. O'Donohoe, b/o play by Maxwell Anderson and Laurence Stallings. Cast: Victor McLaglen, Edmund Lowe, Dolores Del Rio, Phyllis Haver, Leslie Fenton.

WINGS. Paramount, 1927. *William Wellman.* Sp: Hope Loring and Louis D. Lighton, b/o story by John Monk Saunders. Cast: Clara Bow, Charles "Buddy" Rogers, Richard Arlen, Gary Cooper.

ALL QUIET ON THE WESTERN FRONT. Universal, 1930. *Lewis Milestone.* Sp: Dell Andrews, Maxwell Anderson and George Abbott, b/o novel by Erich Maria Remarque. Cast: Lew Ayres, Slim Summerville, Louis Wolheim, John Wray, Ben Alexander.

THE DAWN PATROL. Warners, 1930. *Howard Hawks.* Sp: Howard Hawks, Dan Totheroh, Seton I. Miller, b/o *The Flight Commander* by John Monk Saunders. Cast: Richard Barthelmess, Douglas Fairbanks, Jr., Neil Hamilton.

HELL'S ANGELS. United Artists, 1930. *Howard Hughes.* Sp: Howard Estabrook and Harry Behn, b/o story by Marshall Neilan and Joseph Moncure March. Cast: Ben Lyon, James Hall, Jean Harlow, Douglas Gilmore.

DUCK SOUP. Paramount, 1933. *Leo McCarey*. Sp: Bert Kalmar and Harry Ruby. Cast: Marx Brothers, Margaret Dumont, Louis Calhern, Raquel Torres, Edgar Kennedy.

LA GRANDE ILLUSION (Grand Illusion). RCA Production, 1937. *Jean Renoir*. Sp: Jean Renoir and Charles Spaak, b/o story by Jean Renoir. Cast: Erich von Stroheim, Jean Gabin, Pierre Fresnay, Dalio.

BLOCKADE. A Walter Wanger Production, released by United Artists. 1938. *William Dieterle*. Sp: John Howard Lawson. Cast: Henry Fonda, Madeleine Carroll, Leo Carrillo, John Halliday.

CONFESSIONS OF A NAZI SPY. Warners, 1939. *Anatole Litvak*. Sp: Milton Krims and John Wexley. Cast: Edward G. Robinson, Paul Lukas, Francis Lederer, Sig Rumann.

THE FIGHTING 69TH. Warners, 1940. *William Keighley*. Sp: Norman Reilly Raine, Fred Niblo, Jr., Dean Franklin. Cast: James Cagney, Pat O'Brien, Dennis Morgan, George Brent.

FOREIGN CORRESPONDENT. A Walter Wanger Production, released by United Artists, 1940. *Alfred Hitchcock*. Sp: Charles Bennett and Joan Harrison. Cast: Joel McCrea, Herbert Marshall, Laraine Day, George Sanders, Albert Basserman.

THE GREAT DICTATOR. A Charles Chaplin Production, released by United Artists, 1940. *Charles Chaplin*. Sp: Charles Chaplin. Cast: Charles Chaplin, Jack Oakie, Paulette Goddard, Reginald Gardiner, Chester Conklin.

THE MORTAL STORM. MGM, 1940. *Frank Borzage*. Sp: Claudine West, Andersen Ellis, and George Froeschel, b/o novel by Phyllis Bottome. Cast: Margaret Sullavan, James Stewart, Robert Young, Frank Morgan, Irene Rich, Bonita Granville.

SERGEANT YORK. Warners, 1941. *Howard Hawks*. Sp: Abem Finkel, Harry Chandlee, Howard Koch, and John Huston, b/o diary of Alvin C. York. Cast: Gary Cooper, Joan Leslie, Walter Brennan, George Tobias, Ward Bond.

IN WHICH WE SERVE. A Two Cities Production released by United Artists, 1942. *Noël Coward and David Lean*. Sp: Noël Coward. Cast: Noël Coward, John Mills, Richard Attenborough, Celia Johnson, Bernard Miles.

MRS. MINIVER. MGM, 1942. *William Wyler*. Sp: Arthur Wimperis, George Froeschel, James Hilton, and Claudine West, b/o book by Jan Struther. Cast: Greer Garson, Walter Pidgeon, Teresa Wright, Dame May Whitty, Richard Ney.

WAKE ISLAND. Paramount, 1942. *John Farrow*. Sp: W.R. Burnett and Frank Butler, b/o records of U.S. Marine Corps. Cast: Brian Donlevy, Robert Preston, William Bendix, Macdonald Carey.

ACTION IN THE NORTH ATLANTIC. Warners, 1943. *Lloyd Bacon*. Sp: John Howard Lawson, A.I. Bezzerides, and W.R. Burnett, b/o story by Guy Gilpatric. Cast: Humphrey Bogart, Raymond Massey, Sam Levene, Alan Hale, Ruth Gordon.

AIR FORCE. Warners, 1943. *Howard Hawks*. Sp: Dudley Nichols. Cast: John Garfield, John Ridgely, Gig Young, Arthur Kennedy, Harry Carey.

BATAAN. MGM, 1943. *Tay Garnett*. Sp: Robert D. Andrews. Cast: Robert Taylor, George Murphy, Lloyd Nolan, Barry Nelson, Robert Walker, Thomas Mitchell.

DESTINATION TOKYO. Warners, 1943. *Delmer Daves*. Sp: Delmer Daves and Albert Maltz, b/o story by Steve Fisher. Cast: Cary Grant, John Garfield, Alan Hale, Dane Clark, Warner Anderson.

GUADALCANAL DIARY. 20th Century-Fox, 1943. *Lewis Seiler*. Sp: Lamar Trotti, b/o book by Richard Tregaskis. Cast: Preston Foster, Lloyd Nolan, William Bendix, Anthony Quinn.

SAHARA. Columbia, 1943. *Zoltan Korda*. Sp: John Howard Lawson and Zoltan Korda, b/o story by Philip MacDonald. Cast: Humphrey Bogart, Bruce Bennett, Rex Ingram, Lloyd Bridges, Dan Duryea.

THE HITLER GANG. Paramount, 1944. *John Farrow*. Sp: Frances Goodrich and Albert Hackett. Cast: Robert Watson, Roman Bohnen, Martin Kosleck, Victor Varconi.

LIFEBOAT. 20th Century-Fox, 1944. *Alfred Hitchcock*. Sp: Jo Swerling, b/o story by John Steinbeck. Cast: Tallulah Bankhead, William Bendix, Walter Slezak, John Hodiak, Canada Lee.

OBJECTIVE, BURMA. Warners, 1944. *Raoul Walsh*. Sp: Ranald MacDougall and Lester Cole, b/o story by Alvah Bessie. Cast: Errol Flynn, George Tobias, Warner Anderson, William Prince.

THE PURPLE HEART. 20th Century-Fox, 1944. *Lewis Milestone*. Sp: Jerome Cady, b/o story by Melville Crossman. Cast: Dana Andrews, Farley Granger, Sam Levene, Richard Conte, Richard Loo.

THIRTY SECONDS OVER TOKYO. MGM, 1944. *Mervyn LeRoy*. Sp: Dalton

Trumbo, b/o book by Captain T.W. Lawson and Robert Considine. Cast: Van Johnson, Robert Walker, Phyllis Thaxter, Robert Mitchum, Spencer Tracy.

THE STORY OF G.I. JOE. A Lester Cowan Production, released by United Artists, 1945. *William Wellman*. Sp: Leopold Atlas, Guy Endore, and Philip Stevenson. Cast: Burgess Meredith, Robert Mitchum, Freddie Steele, Wally Cassell.

THEY WERE EXPENDABLE. MGM, 1945. *John Ford*. Sp: Frank Wead, b/o book by William L. White. Cast: Robert Montgomery, John Wayne, Donna Reed, Ward Bond.

A WALK IN THE SUN. 20th Century-Fox, 1945. *Lewis Milestone*. Sp: Robert Rossen, b/o novel by Harry Brown. Cast: Dana Andrews, Richard Conte, Sterling Holloway, Lloyd Bridges.

BATTLEGROUND. MGM, 1949. *William Wellman*. Sp: Robert Pirosh. Cast: Van Johnson, Ricardo Montalban, John Hodiak, George Murphy, Marshall Thompson.

COMMAND DECISION. MGM, 1949. *Sam Wood*. Sp: William R. Laidlaw and George Froeschel, b/o play by William Wister Haines. Cast: Clark Gable, Walter Pidgeon, Van Johnson, Brian Donlevy, Edward Arnold.

TWELVE O'CLOCK HIGH. 20th Century-Fox, 1950. *Henry King*. Sp: Sy Bartlett and Beirne Lay, Jr., b/o their novel. Cast: Gregory Peck, Dean Jagger, Gary Merrill, Hugh Marlowe, Millard Mitchell.

THE DESERT FOX. 20th Century-Fox, 1951. *Henry Hathaway*. Sp: Nunnally Johnson, b/o book by Brigadier Desmond Young. Cast: James Mason, Cedric Hardwicke, Everett Sloane, Leo G. Carroll, Jessica Tandy.

THE STEEL HELMET. Lippert Pictures, Inc., 1951. *Samuel Fuller*. Sp: Samuel Fuller. Cast: Gene Evans, Steve Brodie, Richard Loo, Robert Hutton.

FROM HERE TO ETERNITY. Columbia, 1953. *Fred Zinnemann*. Sp: Daniel Taradash, b/o novel by James Jones. Cast: Burt Lancaster, Montgomery Clift, Deborah Kerr, Frank Sinatra, Donna Reed, Ernest Borgnine.

STALAG 17. Paramount, 1953. *Billy Wilder*. Sp: Billy Wilder and Edwin Blum, b/o play by Donald Bevan and Edmund Trzcinski. Cast: Willian Holden, Otto Preminger, Robert Strauss, Don Taylor, Sig Rumann.

THE CAINE MUTINY. Columbia, 1954. (c). *Edward Dymtryk*. Sp: Stanley Roberts, b/o novel by Herman Wouk. Cast: Humphrey Bogart, Jose Ferrer, Van Johnson, Fred MacMurray, Robert Francis.

THE BRIDGES AT TOKO-RI. Paramount, 1955. (c). *Mark Robson*. Sp: Valentine Davies, b/o novel by James A. Michener. Cast: William Holden, Grace Kelly, Fredric March, Mickey Rooney.

ATTACK! A Robert Aldrich Production, released by United Artists, 1956. *Robert Aldrich*. Sp: James Poe, b/o play *Frail Fox* by Norman Brooks. Cast: Jack Palance, Eddie Albert, Lee Marvin, Richard Jaeckel.

CHINA GATE. A Globe Enterprises Production, released by 20th Century-Fox, 1957. *Samuel Fuller*. Sp: Samuel Fuller. Cast: Gene Barry, Angie Dickinson, Nat (King) Cole, Lee Van Cleef.

NO TIME FOR SERGEANTS. Warners, 1958. *Mervyn LeRoy*. Sp: John Lee Mahin, b/o play by Ira Levin and novel by Mac Hyman. Cast: Andy Griffith, Myron McCormick, Nick Adams, Don Knotts.

PATHS OF GLORY. A Bryna Production, released by United Artists, 1957. *Stanley Kubrick*. Sp:Stanley Kubrick, Calder Willingham and Jim Thompson, b/o novel by Humphrey Cobb. Cast: Kirk Douglas, Adolphe Menjou, Ralph Meeker, George Macready, Wayne Morris.

THE YOUNG LIONS. 20th Century-Fox, 1958. *Edward Dmytryk*. Sp: Edward Anhalt, b/o novel by Irwin Shaw. Cast: Montgomery Clift, Dean Martin, Marlon Brando, Maximilian Schell, Hope Lange.

THE GALLANT HOURS. A Cagney-Montgomery Production, released by United Artists, 1960. *Robert Montgomery*. Sp: Beirne Lay, Jr., Frank D. Gilroy. Cast: James Cagney, Richard Jaeckel, Dennis Weaver, Ward Costello.

THE LONGEST DAY. 20th Century-Fox, 1962. *Ken Annakin, Andrew Marton, Bernhard Wicki*. Sp: Cornelius Ryan, Romain Gary, James Jones, David Pursall, Jack Seddon, b/o book by Cornelius Ryan. Cast: John Wayne, Robert Mitchum, Henry Fonda, Red Buttons, Richard Burton, Rod Steiger.

THE AMERICANIZATION OF EMILY. A Martin Ransohoff Production, released by MGM, 1964. *Arthur Hiller*. Sp: Paddy Chayevsky, b/o novel by William Bradford Huie. Cast: James Garner, Julie Andrews, Melvyn Douglas, James Coburn, Joyce Grenfell.

DR. STRANGELOVE. Columbia, 1964. *Stanley Kubrick*. Sp: Stanley Kubrick, Terry Southern, and Peter George, b/o novel *Red Alert* by Peter George. Cast: Peter Sellers, George C. Scott, Sterling Hayden, Slim Pickens.

THE BLUE MAX. 20th Century-Fox, 1966. (c). *John Guillermin*. Sp: Gerald Hanley, David Pursall, and Jack Seddon, b/o novel by Jack D. Hunter. Cast: George Peppard, James Mason, Ursula Andress.

THE DIRTY DOZEN. A Kenneth Hyman Production, released by MGM, 1967. (c). *Robert Aldrich*. Sp: Nunnally Johnson and Lukas Heller, b/o novel by E.M. Nathanson. Cast: Lee Marvin, Charles Bronson, Jim Brown, John Cassavetes, Richard Jaeckel, Ernest Borgnine.

THE GREEN BERETS. A Batjac Production, released by Warner Bros.-Seven Arts, 1968. (c). *John Wayne, Ray Kellogg*. Sp: James Lee Barrett, b/o novel by Robin Moore. Cast: John Wayne, David Janssen, Jim Hutton, Aldo Ray.

SHAME ("Skammen"). Ingmar Bergman Film for Svensk Filmindustri, 1968. *Ingmar Bergman*. Sp: Ingmar Bergman. Cast: Liv Ullman, Max von Sydow, Gunnar Bjornstrand.

CATCH-22. Paramount, 1970. (c). *Mike Nichols*. Sp: Buck Henry, b/o novel by Joseph Heller. Cast: Alan Arkin, Martin Balsam, Richard Benjamin, Tony Perkins, Jon Voight, Orson Welles.

M*A*S*H. 20th Century-Fox, 1970. (c). *Robert Altman*. Sp: Ring Lardner, Jr., b/o novel by Richard Hooker. Cast: Donald Sutherland, Elliott Gould, Sally Kellerman, Robert Duvall.

PATTON. 20th Century-Fox, 1970. (c). *Franklin J. Schaffner*. Sp: Francis Ford Coppola and Edmund H. North, b/o material from *Patton: Ordeal and Triumph* by Ladislas Farago and *A Soldier's Story* by Omar Bradley. Cast: George C. Scott, Karl Malden, Michael Strong.

INDEX

158

ABOUT THE AUTHOR

Norman Kagan has written for *The Village Voice, Filmmakers Newsletter*, and *Cinema*. He is the author of *The Cinema of Stanley Kubrick*, and taught at Fairleigh Dickinson University and College of New Rochelle. He is a Ph.D. candidate in film at Columbia University.

ABOUT THE EDITOR

Ted Sennett is the author of *Warner Brothers Presents*, a survey of the great Warner films of the Thirties and Forties, and of *Lunatics and Lovers*, on the years of the "screwball" movie comedy. He has also written about films for magazines and newspapers. He lives in New Jersey with his wife and three children.